THINKING DIFFERENTLY

THINKING DIFFERENTLY

*How to **Thrive** Using Your*

Nonlinear Creative Thinking

By Jan Thomas

Copyright © 2020 by Jan Thomas
All rights reserved

For information about permissions to reproduce sections from this book, translation rights, to order bulk purchases, other inquiries, or to contact the author, please go to thinkingdifferentlybook.com

Thomas, Jan
Thinking Differently
How to Thrive Using Your Nonlinear Creative Thinking
ISBN 978-0-578-66855-0
Available in e-book format.

CereCore is a Registered Trademark of CereCore Inc.
FLEX and Insight Change Model are Service Marks of Jan Thomas
www.cerecore.com

Content Categories:
Business & Economics / Leadership
Business & Economics / Personal Success
Education / Learning Styles
Science / Cognitive Science
Self-Help/ Communication & Social Skills

Printed in the U.S.A.
Distributed by Ingram

To Brodye, Hazel, and Kenzie,

*who welcome me into their world
of boundless curiosity, creativity,
and the magic of learning.*

Contents

Introduction 1

Part 1: What Makes a Nonlinear Thinker Different?

Chapter 1 Distinction: Orientation to the World 9

Chapter 2 Distinction: Motivation. 23

Chapter 3 Distinction: Perception of Time 31

Chapter 4 Distinction: Style of Communication 41

Part 2: Leveraging Your Nonlinear Thinking

Chapter 5 Advantages and Opportunities 51

Chapter 6 Classic Roadblocks 63

Part 3: Orchestrate Life Easily and Confidently

Chapter 7 Breaking Away from Prescriptive Strategies. 77

Chapter 8 Flex to Change the Playing Field 87

Chapter 9 Why this Works:
　　　　　　The Science Behind FLEX Strategies 107

Chapter 10 Authentic Self-Advocacy 121

Afterword 133

Acknowledgments 135

Resources 139

Introduction

Knowing what you think is important.
Knowing *how* you think can set you free.

Why do I say that?

Most people think thinking is just thinking. Even though we understand that we may have different viewpoints, it never seems to occur to us that HOW we think may have more to do with how we see the world than even our viewpoints. The fact is, how we think defines the shape of our lives and our communications with others in significant ways.

Just as we are all unique individuals who look different, we think differently, too.

Some people have a sense that they think differently, but they can't identify how. Those people are often creative, visionary, and amazing problem-solvers with unique talents. In companies, teams and individually, I've helped thinkers like these leverage their talents for over 20 years. In working with these clients, there's one major characteristic they have in common: they think in a nonlinear way.

You may have a sense that you think differently, but maybe you don't know that a core part of that uniqueness is not just your talent or skill but the way you think. To show you what I mean, here's an everyday example that might strike a familiar chord. The questions that follow it can help you clarify your own thinking approach.

Jen is a dynamic, accomplished professional woman. Highly organized, she likes orderly, streamlined processes. She can quickly assess a situation and take charge in a way that makes reaching a resolution seem like a foregone conclusion.

Jen's mother, Rebecca, is a talented artist and writer. She went to visit Jen.

After Rebecca arrived, she decided to prepare a special dinner for her working daughter. But the next day when Jen opened her spice drawer — she stared at it!

"Mom, did you do something with the spices?"

"Well, yes," her mom said. "I found the cinnamon, but the nutmeg and ginger were nowhere nearby. I couldn't make sense of it, so I put all the sweet spices together and the herbs together."

"They were in alphabetical order, Mom. You rearranged them by flavor?" Jen laughed. "How am I supposed to find anything?" she asked.

"I drew you a map right here, see?" replied Rebecca.

Telling the story, Jen still laughs. "That is *so* Mom!"

Rebecca's taste map is a perfect example of *nonlinear intelligence* — the subject of this book. It's a form of natural intelligence found in a minority of the population. The central characteristic is a unique kind of thought called *nonlinear thinking*.

If you think you might be a nonlinear thinker, what clues might give you an answer?

When you start a new project or adventure …

- Do you like to step back and see the big picture before jumping in — and enjoy finding connections that create a whole array of new ideas?
- Are you curious and love a challenge?
- Are you motivated more by what inspires you than by external rewards?
- Are you optimistic (sometimes overly so) about how much you can accomplish in a set period of time?
- Do you sometimes find words limiting and too slow to keep up with your thoughts?

If any of these characteristics sounds familiar, it's likely you're a nonlinear thinker. And if you are, you're a member of an evolving group of original thinkers. It turns out that as a nonlinear thinker (let's say an "NL thinker" to save time), you engage the world in a whole different way *simply because of how you think*.

That nonlinear orientation gives you access to talents that are especially well-suited for today's world of uncertainty and change. In short, you're in exactly the right place at the right time.

But the wonders of nonlinear thinking don't come without challenges. That's because most organizations and systems, from corporations to schools, are built from the linear approach, an approach that's often also called prescriptive. And it's all too familiar to nonlinear thinkers, who sometimes struggle to navigate in these environments. In prescriptive settings, problems are attacked step by step, communication is detailed and documented in writing, and time is managed and measured for efficiency.

As an NL thinker, your natural tendencies are the exact opposite. You're swimming against the current.

This book shows you how to actually move with the current — not by eschewing your inherent talents and adopting "the ways of the world" but by embracing your gifts and leveraging them in a whole new way. This allows you to function at your highest level and work in harmony with how you think, unleashing far more of your mind's amazing power while also giving you less stress and more enjoyment.

Long before writing this book, I discovered the importance of understanding and harmonizing with how we think — I'm an NL myself. At age 6, I dreamed of being a ballerina.

I imagined myself costumed in fluffy pink, rhythmically floating across the floor, across the stage, around the world. My mother enrolled me in ballet class. With no music playing, we stood in line. The teacher called out commands: "Ten steps to the right! Five steps to the left! Repeat four times!"

Everyone was moving left while I was still moving right.

"STOP! Start again." Repetition didn't help. There'd be no tutus, no satin toe shoes, no floating for me.

I gave up ballet. I gave up the idea of ever being a dancer — until I signed up for a college modern dance class. The teacher greeted us with a drum in her hand and started beating a rhythm. "Move to the rhythm you hear," she said. No counting, no rules, just free-floating, self-choreographed movement. I loved it.

As it turns out, I am *not* a klutz. I'm just an NL thinker. My nonlinear thinking style didn't make me incapable of learning ballet, but I certainly wasn't good at following and remembering a series of verbal instructions.

When asked to spontaneously move to a drumbeat, I could glide around the floor. I remembered and easily repeated the steps at subsequent classes. I remember them to this day — I was in harmony with my natural way of learning, but I didn't know it at the time.

This experience stayed in my mind and triggered my curiosity. I wanted to know why my second dance experience was so different from my (painful) first one.

Ultimately, this became an intense professional quest to discover all I could about how people learn, including the new findings in cognitive neuroscience, the study of how the brain works. My efforts culminated in the formation of CereCore Institute, an organization that specializes in services for NL thinkers.

To clarify something here, what we call *nonlinear thinking* is an umbrella term, not a single style. No two nonlinear thinkers share exactly the same configuration of thinking processes and talents. Every NL is unique, emphasizing an individual constellation of processes and talents while sharing some universal NL thinking characteristics.

And while we distinguish NL thinking from linear thinking, there are lots of ways to process information — both for linear and nonlinear thinkers — and depending on the need, these processes often intertwine. But there are fundamental differences between linear and nonlinear thinkers, which we'll identify in these chapters.

Once we began our work with nonlinear thinkers, it wasn't long before they started asking for a book that could be their reference and guide. Their encouragement — and at times their insistence — led to my writing *Thinking Differently*.

And they had demands for this guide: it couldn't be too long, needed lots of graphics and plenty of real-life stores. A good challenge. So in this book their wishes are granted.
- The graphics are used purposely to organize key information *visually* so you as a reader can get the information *rapidly* without long explanations.
- The Graphic Chapter Overviews just at the beginning of each chapter give you the *big picture,* demonstrating the relationship of the points

made in the chapter. Some readers like to have an overview in mind while reading a chapter while others prefer to read the chapter first and then refer back to the overview.
- First-person stories offering examples of NL thinking are frequent.
- But the words are minimal so NLs can focus on the overall concepts.

In a compact, approachable format, the book distills mulitple layers of neuroscience, behavioral research and testing. It identifies what nonlinear thinking looks like; it helps you leverage your unique thinking talents by introducing a new set of strategies that enable you to navigate the landscape of your everyday nonlinear life. *Thinking Differently* doesn't tell you what to do or how to explore: it's a guide for your self-directed, creative journey.

Thinking Differently is divided into three parts:

- **Part 1, WHAT MAKES A NONLINEAR THINKER DIFFERENT**, introduces the Four Distinctions that describe nonlinear thinkers. Understanding these Distinctions has the potential to transform your life.
- **Part 2, LEVERAGING YOUR NONLINEAR THINKING**, considers the gifts and opportunities that come with being an NL thinker and the key ways to leverage those strengths and minimize limiting factors.
- **Part 3, ORCHESTRATE LIFE EASILY AND CONFIDENTLY**, shows you how to overcome the restrictive strategies we've all been taught and offers you new neuroscience-based strategies that instantly and easily help NL thinkers do things *their way*. These strategies allow you to work *with*, not against, your natural tendencies.

Thinking Differently is filled with examples of nonlinear thinkers who've learned that, while being NL means being different, *this difference* is really a distinct gift that takes their thinking to a new level.

They have moved to become the confident conductor of their lives, harmonizing their natural thinking with how they want to live instead of playing from the position of "first chair," as good as that is. This book is both a tool and a reminder that, armed with understanding and with strategies organic to your natural nonlinear approach, you can thrive as never before, and the symphony you create can soar.

Thinking Differently

PART 1

What Makes a Nonlinear Thinker Different?

Thinking Differently

CHAPTER 1

First NL Distinction

Orientation to the World

"To be a champion, I think you have to see the big picture."

— **Summer Sanders,**
Olympic gold medal swimmer, sports commentator, actress

Graphic Chapter Overview

The nonlinear thinking process

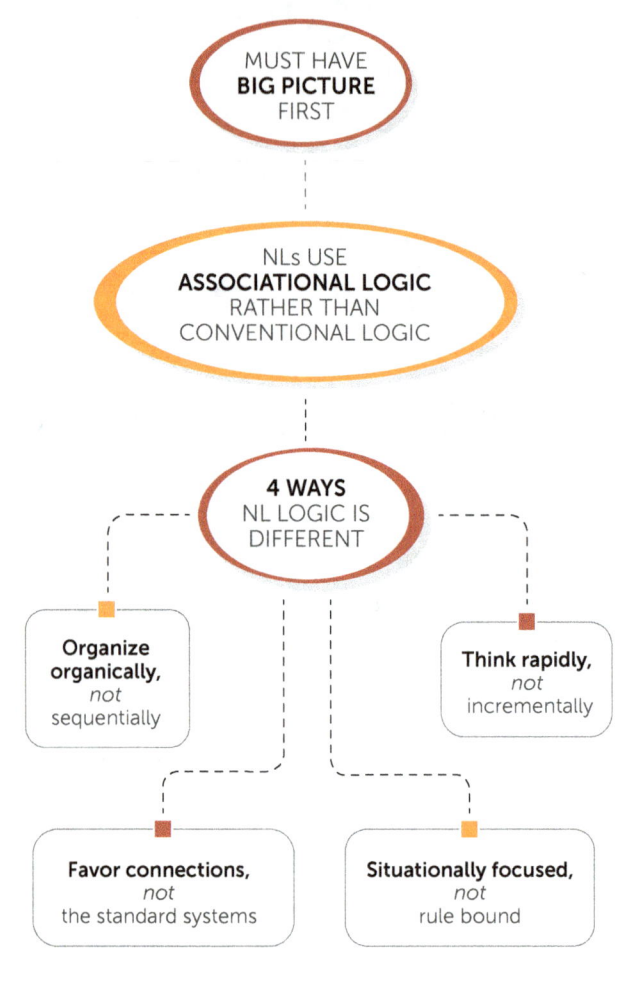

Dave is a CPA and financial planner. He's also a nonlinear thinker. When new clients come to him for financial advice and want to get right into the specifics, *instead* he takes a different approach. He hits the brakes and asks a lot of questions about the clients' goals, dreams, family, and short- and long-range plans. He does that because he wants to see *the big picture* and understand the entire *context* of his clients' concerns.

Dave's approach is somewhat like a doctor diagnosing a patient's entire set of symptoms and seeing the big picture before proceeding to treatment. If the doctor had to isolate and gather data sequentially from each one of the 37.2 trillion cells in a patient's body, she'd be overwhelmed by the sheer volume of data. Instead, she begins by creating an overview, by taking vital signs and observing the patient's key symptoms.

Similarly, when a detective arrives at a murder scene, he first steps back and looks over the entire scene — the physical environment, the orientation and condition of the body, and possible suspects — to get the whole picture. He then gathers evidence, reconstructing events as fully as possible, and fits them into his puzzle. All his preliminary work helps establish context and give him the big picture — just as it does for the doctor and Dave.

Regardless of the vocation or task, nonlinear and linear thinkers process information in different ways, using different, invisible priorities. For linear thinkers to understand, they need to see the details first and build their big picture from them. Nonlinear thinkers — NLs — look to see the big picture first and work in the variety of details as they make sense to that larger view.

The Big Picture and Context

For NL thinkers, the big picture is fundamental to understanding the world and any task before them. It's not enough to have the big picture revealed to them at the end because, without the big picture, NLs don't know where to put the details — or how to put order to what's presented to them.

> *"I get bombarded with all this detail before it has any meaning for me, and I don't have anywhere in my mind to put it. So, it goes in one ear and out the other."*
> —**Dave**, *client*

Looking at the whole picture first does take extra time. So an NL may sometimes seem to be wasting time or slow. But you aren't slow. In fact, you frequently arrive at the solution first. That's because — *before you take action* — you take the time to orient yourself to the whole context.

Your relationship to the whole is the key.

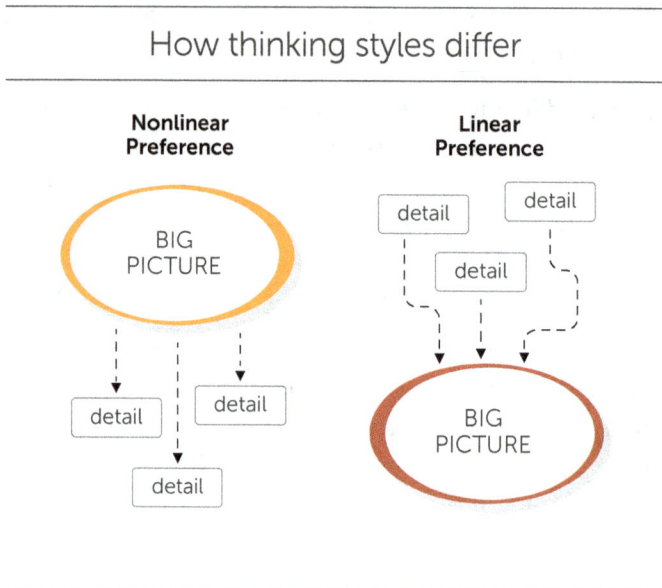

Nonlinear thinkers remember details when they start with the big picture first.

Here's how Dave describes it: "The core thing for me is to get the big picture before I can do anything else. When I work with clients, I'm always interested in what's motivating their questions, what they are really asking. Often there's something underneath driving their question.

"It's like an iceberg, where what you see above the water is only a fraction of the whole thing. My goal is to see and understand as much of the whole picture as possible because that's the context that will reveal the most complete solution.

"It's when I have access to the whole iceberg that I can see the relationships and make the connections that make all the difference."

Dave recognizes now how his natural nonlinear orientation not only affects his approach to his work but also shaped his experience as a student in high school.

"I'm most engaged when I'm learning about one thing — but within its broadest context. For example, if I'm reading about history, I want to know the context of what's going on at the same time in the art, politics, and economics of the period. This lets me make connections that make sense to me and helps me remember. If I don't have those things, I have difficulty relating to and remembering information."

Iceberg thinking

Back in high school, Dave rarely got the full picture. So, he couldn't make the connections that help him get inspired. As a result, he did just enough to get by — because without a puzzle to solve, it all seemed formulaic and limiting, not enough of a challenge. He wanted to find out new things. He loved the challenge when a solution was uncertain. Without that, he just cruised.

This need for the big picture requires its own logic; a way of thinking and problem-solving that's both unconventional and, for NLs like Dave, wholly natural.

NLs' Associational Logic

Traditionally, logic is considered to be analytical and sequential. It arrives at conclusions by following a methodical, linear series of deductions. When Dave sees his clients' questions as an iceberg, he uses an entirely different kind of logic, one that's intrinsic to NL thinking.

This associational logic is what allows NLs to be highly gifted as creative problem-solvers and visionary communicators. And this nonlinear logic is based on making previously undetected connections among seemingly unrelated elements.

This kind of thought process releases explosions of energy similar to the rapid synaptic firing of the brain when it's learning something exciting. Making associational connections creates breakthroughs that are multi-directional, multi-dimensional, and virtually instantaneous.

How did Wilbur and Orville Wright discover the secret of controlled flight? The story goes that while Wilbur was talking with a customer in their bicycle shop, he was holding a small cardboard box. As he talked, he idly twisted the box in his hands.

The slight warping of the flat surfaces reminded Wilbur of something — buzzard wings! He'd seen buzzards gently twist their wings to soar on thermal updrafts.

Suddenly, he understood the answer to the centuries-old mystery of controlled flight. All he and Orville had to do was figure out a way to warp the plane's wings to create something similar.

The brothers designed wires that would give the pilot manual control of wing warping so the pilot could actually steer the plane. Wilbur's associative leap from box to bird to the critical roll control of airplane wings was hardly a straight line of logic. But his associational logic solved a problem that had stumped everyone before him.

NL thinkers are in a continual state of associating. It comes naturally from their big-picture orientation. Relationships and connections don't emerge when we focus only on the obvious details right in front of us. It's like the iceberg. Expanding the view to include not just the obvious but also everything below the surface allows us to see relationships and make critical connections not evident previously.

For NLs, creating associations among the diverse objects, actions, people, and events around them doesn't stop with the present moment. Past associations and future potentialities can easily be in the mix.

So, don't assume that that faraway look on the face of an NL friend is empty daydreaming. You might actually be witnessing unique connections being made in another mental time zone.

Associational thinking frees NLs from trying to fit their unique logic into standard, sequential threads of thought that don't serve their natural

First NL Distinction: Orientation to the World

approach. Nonlinear, associational logic is distinctly different from the common linear method in four principal ways.

The Four Features of Associational Logic

1. Organically Ordered

Nonlinear, associational thinking is organically, not sequentially, ordered.

The trunk of a tree might appear to spring vertically from the soil and grow upward until it reaches its natural height. But the tree is always growing multi-directionally and multi-dimensionally. As the trunk and branches grow above ground, the roots grow downward and outward. The "vertical" tree is really a spherical life form.

Associational thinking is invisibly and organically ordered in the way that a tree's growth is organically structured.

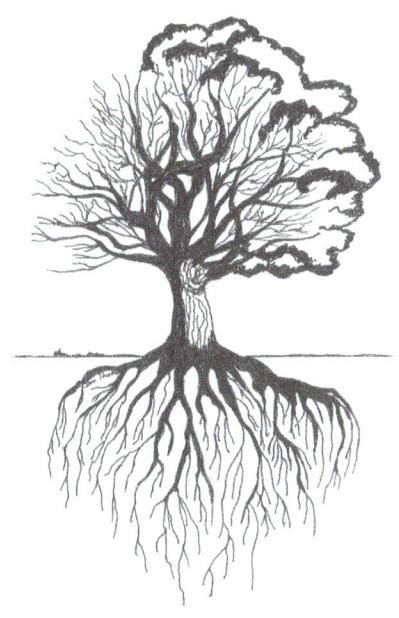

The NL's associational thinking and big-picture view expand in all directions at once. Reaching out in every direction, the NL mind receives input from all kinds of sources, pursues ideas in all kinds of sequences, and is able to arrive at creative solutions that aren't apparent to others.

Having your mind go rapidly in all directions at once may seem like an invitation to complication. Actually, it can open the NL thinker to remarkable simplicity.

I have two friends, Lara and Tom, who each love to cook. But when it comes to how they go about it, they're a study in contrast. It's a perfect expression of

Thinking Differently

how each one thinks. Lara takes a linear approach; Tom goes nonlinear.

Lara says she starts preparing for our holiday dinner with a list. Several days before the gathering, she types up the entire menu. She also includes all the ingredients with the amounts and sequence of their combination, plus a description and timetable for each step, and then the procedures, including the temperatures and durations, as well as the precise time the food is to be plated. The dinner she served was delicious.

Tom also invited us to dinner over the holidays. On the day of the meal, he put on his apron and headed to the kitchen to draw out a plan. First, he made a list of the items on his menu. Then with a few quick strokes he made some vertical and horizontal lines, added a few instructions and reminders — and set the pen down.

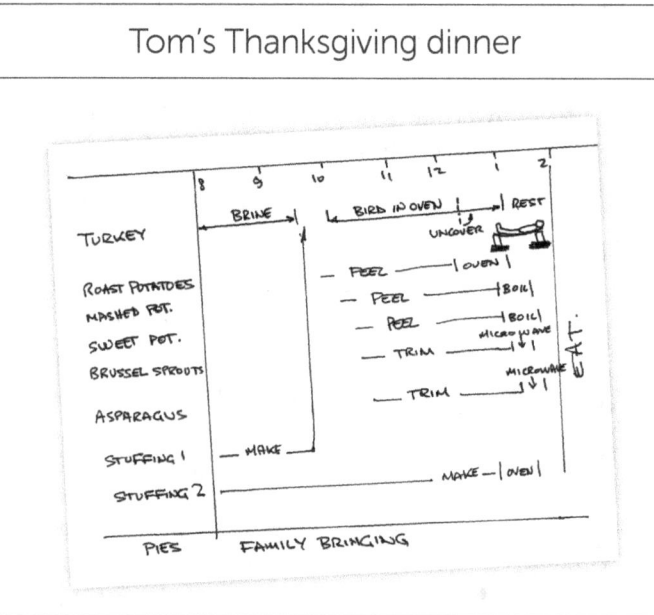

Tom saw creating the meal visually as a reminder of what was going on in his mind, a creation of ingredients and timing.

Tom's timing-oriented chart has food listed on the left and time across the top. The rest of the page shows periods of time when food needs to be prepared or checked.

This is all the information Tom needs or wants! Anything more, he insists, would distract him. The chart gives him the big picture, the few keywords serving as triggers that remind him of all the associated plans and tasks that he keeps in his head. We had another fantastic meal.

Many NL thinkers start with even less structure, randomly writing down ideas on a whiteboard or notepad as they occur without trying to assemble them in any particular sequence. Maybe you've done this kind of nonspecific download of ideas. If so, you're in good company. A lot of our clients claim at this point, "Oh, so *that's* what's going on in my head!" By getting their thoughts out of their minds and in visual form, they can see relationships and make connections for understanding and action.

2. Associational Rather Than Conventional Logic

An NL's associational thinking is so rapid that it defies conventional logic.

Wilbur Wright's manipulating a cardboard box wasn't a controlled experiment in aerodynamics. It was a seemingly random, unrelated act. But when he saw the semirigid structure of the box flex in his hands, his mind associated that with the way he'd seen birds bend their wings in the air currents. That mental picture allowed him to make the intuitive leap to the solution for roll control in an airplane.

His solution wasn't logical by the usual definition. But it made perfect sense ... and history! Associational logic fits the nonlinear thinker's need for the big picture — and what the context reveals — because it frees the mind to consider a whole array of connections, relationships, and possibilities.

3. Situational Rather Than Rule-Based Logic

Associational thinking has no set rules to follow in the traditional sense.

It is a toolbox, with the primary tools being these: pattern recognition, cross-disciplinary thinking, and visual modeling. But there's no prescription for which tools to include, which ones have to be used where, or in which order. It's all up to the discretion of the user and the dictates of the situation. It's an exploratory, creative process. You are in charge.

Thinking Differently

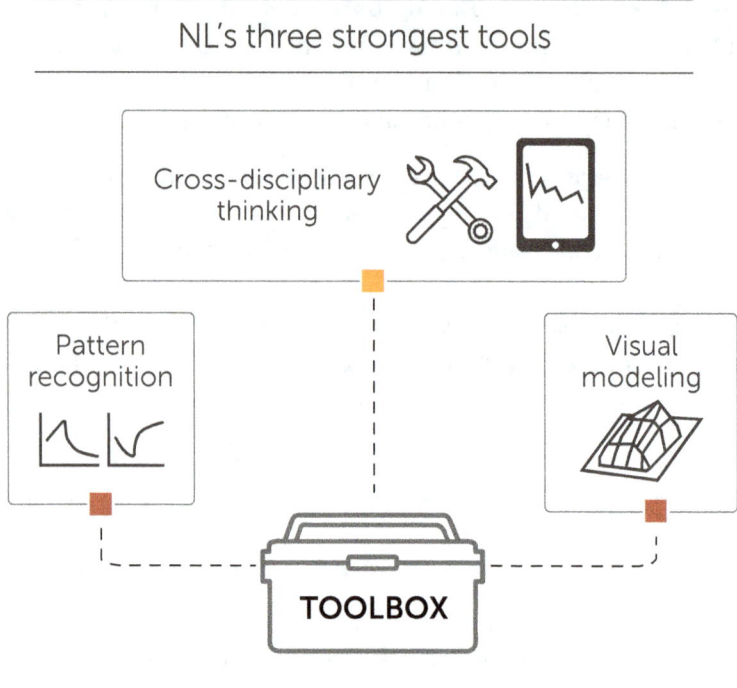

Three flexible tools support NL thinking, depending on the situation.

Jordan is an aerospace engineer and an avid fly fisherman. Before he reported to his first job, he rewarded himself with a fishing trip to New Zealand.

Wading into the Greenstone River on the South Island, he noticed a constantly shifting world — subtle changes in the speed and depth of the water, contours of the eddies, intensity of sunlight and shade, flashes of concealed trout. "I had no guide to tell me which fly to use or which section of river to fish. I had to think through variables and figure out the key things I needed to do. So, I changed fishing techniques as the situation changed." Jordan watched for patterns, adjusted his position, and chose his flies based on conditions.

The changing conditions of the weather and the river were his guide. What seemed a big complex problem for him was fun to solve. The ability to creatively adapt in the moment is at the core of Jordan's definition for when he has fished well. It's also the essence of associational logic in action.

4. Rapid, Not Incremental Solutions

Nonlinear, associational thinking develops rapidly and multi-directionally.

At lightning speed, the brain's synapses connect multiple disciplines, inputs, and relationships — including many in the subconscious — until the critical combination coalesces and bursts out into insight.

The great mathematician and physicist Archimedes had been tasked with assessing the precise weight of gold in the king's ornate crown without damaging it. One day as he stepped into his bath, Archimedes noticed how his bathwater rose as he entered.

He suddenly knew the solution of how to safely weigh the king's crown. It's said he was so excited that he bolted down the street dripping wet and stark naked to tell the king. Today, Archimedes' Principle is a law of physics that is fundamental to fluid mechanics: the upward buoyant force exerted on a body immersed in a fluid is equal to the weight of the fluid that the body displaces.

Nonlinear thinking does not proceed incrementally.

It considers multiple inputs, observations, and information over time, letting these stir and ferment until the right relationships connect, leading to leaps in knowledge and new ways of doing things.

How can we prepare for such catalytic moments? We do it by simply maintaining an open state of readiness.

Wilbur Wright bent a cardboard box; Archimedes took a bath.

Summary

A defining characteristic of nonlinear thinkers is the desire to start with the big picture. In order to engage with the world, your associational mind works rapidly to recognize patterns and relationships, making unlikely but insightful connections. In a sense, you are like a detective finding patterns and connections.

How NL thinkers are like detectives.

DETECTIVES	NL THINKERS
Start with a challenge and unknown	Attracted to challenge and unknown
Use observation to create the big picture	Find big picture by looking for similar/dissimilar patterns
Ask wide-ranging questions, follow curiosity	Ask questions — many seemingly unrelated to deepen the back story
Use visual board/screen to see known facts	Use visual board/screen to see connections and relationships
Build possible scenarios	Identify several possibilities
Synthesize all data	Synthesize options
Solve the crime	Choose the best option for a solution

In their problem-solving, nonlinear thinkers are like detectives.

According to Peter Russell in The Brain Book, there are an estimated 10 billion neurons in the human brain — as many as there are stars in the Milky Way. And each neuron can make over 10,000 connections! As an NL thinker, your brain excels at rapid-fire connectivity. It supports your strengths: keen observational skills, ability to synthesize disparate data, a talent for visual modeling, and spatial intelligence.

How we think isn't about which method we like better. How we think depends on how we're wired. Your big-picture view is a defining distinction of your associational NL thinking style, and it shapes how you engage with your world. Good news: we're living in a time that's especially well-suited to your big-picture thinking approach.

With the big picture in mind, the next question is, "What motivates you?" ||

First NL Distinction: Orientation to the World

Thinking Differently

CHAPTER 2

Second NL Distinction

Motivation

> *"Passion is energy. Feel the power that comes from focusing on what excites you."*
> — **Oprah Winfrey**
> *TV host, entrepreneur*

Graphic Chapter Overview

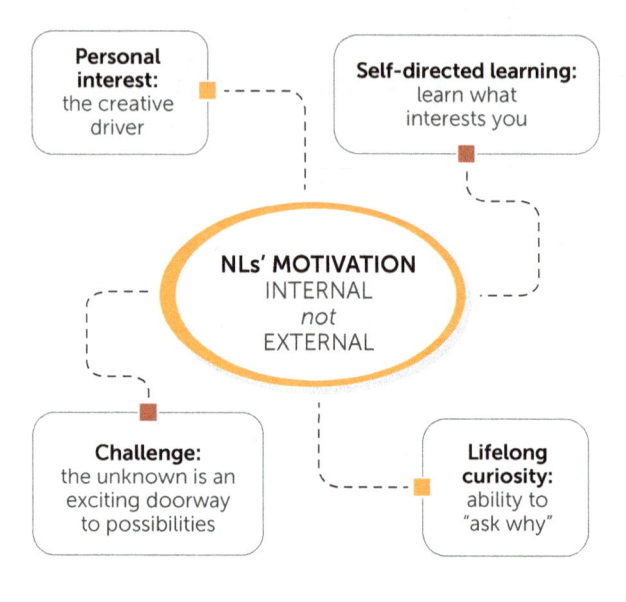

Having interesting ideas is invigorating, but transforming those ideas into realities takes action — not just once, but with sustained follow-through. That takes motivation.

The second distinction of NL thinkers is motivation — what moves you. And what doesn't. What is not at the top of that list is money, awards, trophies, and fame. If these things come your way, that is OK, but your primary motivations are internal rather than external.

> "Once something is a passion, the motivation is there."
>
> — **Michael Schumacher,**
> seven-time Formula One world champion race car driver

What fires you up are things that interest you personally, regardless of what anyone else says should be your focus. Understanding that fact, using it as a cornerstone to build your life, has the power to transform everything you do. And how you do it.

Self-Directed Learning

Nonlinear thinkers learn what interests them. Even as a 10-year-old, Greg liked finding out how things worked. From computing hardware to the lawn mower to how the family dog managed to get out of the fenced yard. Greg dedicated his imagination to investigating — but only in his own way.

That meant lots of building projects. Cars, rockets, and airplanes became his laboratory of self-directed learning. His long-suffering parents eventually gave him a room in the house to store his creations.

His self-directed approach to learning also got him in trouble at school.

"If I wasn't interested, it was very hard for me to remember things, and that included homework. I always felt bad about it, but I still wouldn't do it," says Greg. "I couldn't make myself do it, no matter what the consequences were. This was confusing to me."

It was confusing to Greg's parents as well. Neither they nor his teachers could find rewards or punishments that would change his behavior. "He's evidently a lot more interested in following his own interests than learning the actual lessons," his teacher says. "He needs to apply himself to his assignments."

The fact that he didn't comply isn't a flaw in Greg's nature or his learning ability. It's simply an indication of his nonlinear thinking. In college, where he had more of a role in choosing what he studied, he began to thrive. Interested in both language and science, he chose a school with a fully integrated liberal arts and science curriculum.

"I loved applying sociology to history or physics to humanities," he says. "I enjoyed finding patterns in non-pattern stuff. For instance, I figured out that every battle fought between smart ground troops on one side and brilliant commanders on the other goes to the ground troops!"

After graduation and some false starts, he finally found work that engaged his personal interests and leveraged his nonlinear gifts. He's the CEO of a thriving full-service internet marketing agency. He reads trends and patterns, discovers anomalies, makes connections, and finds how things work most effectively for a diverse group of clients.

Greg's lifelong pursuit of how things work also points to another of the classic motivating forces that drive NLs' passion — curiosity. Things fascinate you, mysteries intrigue you, uncertainty and the unknown excite you.

Lifelong Curiosity

> *"If it's a cliché to say that intellectual curiosity keeps your mind sharp, your senses alert, and your capabilities cutting-edge, that's because it's true."*
>
> — **Adena Friedman,**
> *president and CEO, Nasdaq*

Anatomy, engineering, hydraulics, geology, geometry, astronomy, music, emotion, and light: this is a short list of subjects Leonardo da Vinci mastered. In his biography of the Renaissance genius, Walter Isaacson noted, "Any man who puts, 'Describe the tongue of a woodpecker' on his to-do list is over-endowed with the combination of curiosity and acuity."

Leonardo's lifelong delight in exploring and integrating everything that fascinated him came to fruition in his painting the Mona Lisa. His studies of light, shadow, and physiology materialized in this painting: no matter where the viewer stands, the eyes of the young Lisa Gherardini appear to follow. Though Leonardo wasn't the first artist to do this, it has come to be known as the "Mona Lisa effect."

Without question, the fact that Leonardo applied the learnings gained from his engaged and eclectic curiosity to his paintings, sculpture, and inventions is what's placed him so prominently in the pantheon of the world's geniuses. But for him, these expressions, however beautifully rendered, were only byproducts. It was the process of exploration and discovery that was his real passion, culminated not in an artistic masterpiece but in the revelation of another avenue to explore.

Excited by the Unknown

NLs challenge themselves. And it's not a form of self-denial, self-doubt, or self- punishment — it's a love of the game. Not knowing the solution to a problem triggers your curiosity. New ideas, solutions, and alternatives beckon. Rather than scaring, frustrating or demoralizing you, they are invitations to see patterns in non-pattern stuff.

Who knows what will become of these invitations, these infinite pattern variations NLs can see?

> *"The challenge of the unknown future is so much more exciting than the stories of the accomplished past."*
> — **Simon Sinek,**
> *author and organizational consultant*

The ability to reframe challenges as opportunities for free-form exploration is one of your greatest gifts as an NL. That attitudinal shift allows you to kick your attention into a higher gear at critical moments. It powers redirection, creative pause, deep listening, visual mapping, and intuitive experimentation.

Summary

Passion is a primary motivator for linear and nonlinear thinkers alike. But what you're passionate about and how you fuel that passion can be very different. For NLs, personal interest, curiosity, and challenge stoke the fires of passion all life long.

We saw this passion in both Greg and Leonardo. Greg built models, took things apart, and made discoveries. He also had to face the consequences of holding to his self-directed learning style even in the face of his prescribed-but-ignored school assignments. As an adult, he's motivated by the same NL passions in his current work, leading a digital marketing agency. Leonardo combined an insatiable curiosity, uncanny powers of observation, and a genius for creative expression into a body of work whose breadth and beauty have inspired the world for 500 years.

One of the unique traits of nonlinear thinking is its close connection to following your emotions. "Follow your heart" could be the defining motto for NLs because it speaks directly to the personal interests and self-directed learning that are so important for you.

As an NL thinker, your passion is your power. Whatever the scope of your quest, the seed of its solution is not out there somewhere. It's right inside you. ||

Second NL Distinction: Motivation

Thinking Differently

CHAPTER 3

Third NL Distinction

Perception of Time

> *"Time and space are modes by which we think and not conditions in which we live."*
> — **Albert Einstein,** *developer of the Theory of Relativity*

Graphic Chapter Overview

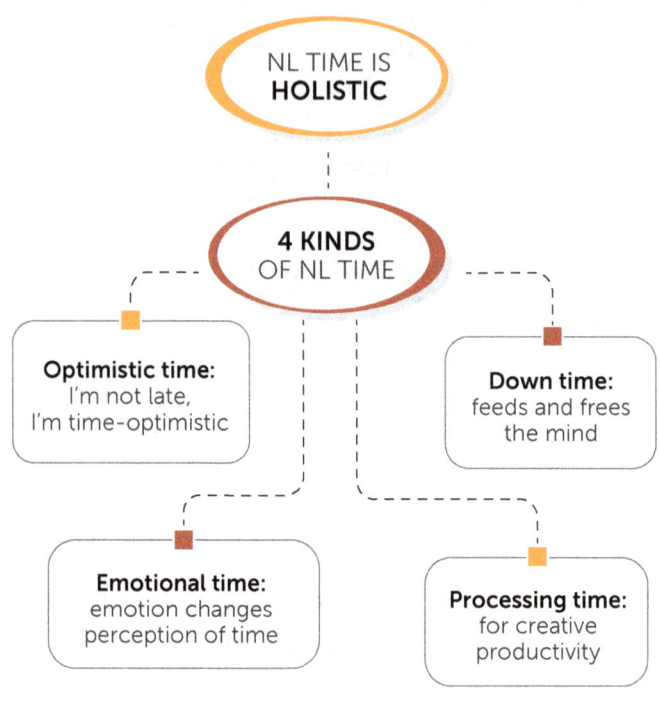

History is often represented with timelines. But for NL thinkers, time is far more flexible than a straight line or even the curved lines of a 24-hour clock. It unfolds in the organic, multi-directional modes of your NL mind. That means it sometimes flows in nonchronological sequences.

The third fundamental distinction of nonlinear thinkers is how you perceive time.

In a way, how you experience time is an extension of your big-picture view and the need for context. NLs see the world as a connected whole. Your natural inclination is to look for those connections and to explore them.

Your sense of time is not segmented, regimented, or linear. It's holistic, not tied to the minute and hour hands but to the whole experience.

Third NL Distinction: Perception of Time

Take, for example, a seemingly simple question like, "When was it that we saw Susan?" Instead of just responding with the date and time, NLs frequently demonstrate remarkable visual-imaging talent. They might answer by detailing the entire tapestry of the event: "The restaurant had very large windows, and I see her wearing a blue dress and leaning on the table. It must have been fall because the sun was setting over the lake and the trees were at the peak of changing color and the light seemed to set the whole forest on fire." The time and date eventually may emerge but rarely first.

Another part of the holistic view of time is that NLs tend to be future-oriented. It's as if once freed of the concept that time is measured only in the sequential march of minutes and hours, you're given permission to entertain the magical possibilities of time itself. Passion and curiosity flow in "what if" scenarios. Unlike the static past, the future is a fluid and enticing, exciting place.

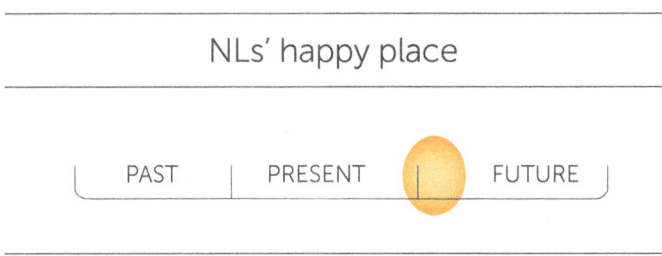

Nonlinear thinkers fluidly move from one time frame to another, but they tend to be future-oriented.

Many NLs are science-fiction buffs, finding time warps and space ripples as natural as breathing. This future orientation within time speaks to your love of exploration, your fascination with the unknown, your willingness to embrace uncertainty.

Here in the linear dominance of Western culture, where deliverables are given not only timelines but deadlines, time is a commodity, something saved, lost, or given an objective value: "Time is money."

In many respects, NLs are more in tune with Eastern culture, where time is subjective, flexible, and can be stretched. A client, Jake, told me that he didn't feel comfortable with what he perceived as the almost constant pressures of time in the U.S. On a hunch, I suggested he might consider taking a vacation in India.

Several months later, I got a call. "I know exactly what you mean now," Jake said.

"I don't like crowds or heat, so my first thought when you suggested I visit India was, 'She's nuts.'"

Jake had just returned from India, and he went on to say, "I felt so at home in New Delhi! At first, it just seemed chaotic. The streets were crowded, hot, and incredibly noisy. But the longer I stayed, the more I could see and feel an order to it. It's not chaos; it's just different. Their time isn't 'the big stick' it usually is to me here. They have this ease with time. It takes as long as it takes for everything to come together. I loved the flexibility. And things still got done!"

In one situation, Jake had asked what hours a local museum was open. He expected a short response. Instead the museum guide started telling him how the Mughals had first come to the area and built a fort, how the different family members ruled, and how agriculture had changed. He talked about local customs and his own family history in the area.

"I thought I was going to get a couple of sentences," Jake said, "and I came away with an entire mini-history of the region. When I went into the museum, I saw the exhibits with completely different eyes because I had a much richer background."

NLs' holistic relationship with time tends to manifest in four primary ways: optimistic time, emotional time, down time, and processing time. Every individual is unique, and all have different levels, combinations, and expressions of these traits. But all four are hallmarks of the NL experience.

1. Optimistic Time

Virtually all NL thinkers share a passion for what interests them and a richly abundant inner life. The combination of these two qualities leads many NLs to be what we call *"time-optimistic."*

Here's a typical NL announcing weekend plans: "I want to get the spare bedroom painted, go to Jill's soccer game, of course go to the landfill to get

Third NL Distinction: Perception of Time

rid of the garden clippings, and definitely see that new movie everyone is talking about. Oh, and I've mapped out where all the new furniture will go — once we get it ordered on Sunday."

... All doable in the mind, so why should it be a problem in time?

For NL thinkers, the mind's ability to do several things instantaneously can be deceptive.

In the mind, every fascinating idea and plan is equally possible and therefore equally valuable. NLs may invest an equal amount of emotional energy in all of them under the flag of, "If it's important, there'll be time for it." Since it's all important, there should be time for everything.

That kind of optimism can get a lot done. It can also create stress, disappointment, and resentment — when it comes up against real-time constraints or conflicts with other people's schedules and priorities.

NLs are 'time-optimistic'

> DONE BY NOON:
> ☑ SET UP INTERVIEW
> ☑ RESEARCH TRIP
> ☑ WALK DOG
> ☑ LAUNDRY
> ☐ WRITE PROPOSAL

I have a friend, Erica, for whom "arrival time" is just a starting place. I'll get a text saying she's running a little late, just leaving her meeting because a couple of things had to be tied up.

A second text lets me know the state of the traffic. A third text joyfully announces that she's coming up the hill to my house ... some 45 minutes later. She runs late for meetings and events even though she always plans (mentally) to be there on time.

Erica isn't oblivious or inconsiderate. She's time-optimistic. Her overconfidence in what can be accomplished springs from her holistic view of time. Her interests and emotion shape how she sees and uses time.

So, even though Erica plans to arrive for dinner at 7 p.m., emotionally she is driven to tie up the loose ends at her meeting. Doing both messes with the time frame, but the two have equal value in Erica's connecting mind. Her perception of time stretches to accommodate both, even though the hands on the clock make no such adjustment.

2. Emotional Time

We sit down "for just a minute" and get so absorbed in what we're doing that an hour or more goes by — without our noticing it. A simple Google search turns into spelunking along semi-related threads. Or time will drag interminably when we're faced with doing taxes.

This is called *emotional time* because our emotional engagement (or lack thereof) changes our perception of time dramatically. Time warp can be commonplace for NL thinkers because they are fascinated and passionate about many things.

> *"My goal with whatever I'm working on is to lose track of time."*
>
> — **Ben Marcus,**
> *author, Columbia University fiction professor*

Before Jake went to India, he worried about a time warp issue at work. "At work I get thinking about a design problem we have, and I lose all track of time. If it was just me, it wouldn't be a problem. But sometimes I've left my team waiting for me while I'm down the hall in some other time zone. I'm embarrassed to waste their time, but my mind, my creative process, just doesn't work in measured blocks of time. If I'm on a roll, it's hard to shift gears even if I *have* noticed the clock."

Are there strategies to work around NLs' time double binds? Yes. We will get to them later in the book.

3. Down Time

NL thinkers need mental down time. The chance to let the mind wander freely or to be still and quiet is not only healthy, NLs desperately need a break from over-stimulation.

Dave, the financial planner, is also a photographer. His office is an eclectic mix of spreadsheets, tax code manuals, framed and unframed photographs, computers, and cameras. He can and does move from working time to *down time* and back again whenever he feels the need to just putter. He likes to take his dog for a walk. He can also escape by selecting a few photographs for the next competition. He may go back and forth from these endeavors several times in a day to keep his mind fresh, clear, and engaged.

> *"I like gardening. It's a place where I find myself when I need to lose myself."*
>
> — **Alice Seybold,**
> *American author*

When Jordan, the aerospace engineer, is in hip boots reading the Greenstone River, it feeds his nonlinear mind while setting it free from structured daily routines.

These are the regenerating benefits of down time. It satisfies the need to explore without additional parameters invading the process. Gardening. Puttering around the house. Tinkering with engines. Browsing outdoor markets. Or simply staring into space ... such *non-doing* is a crucial part of effective doing! It's the breathing in that allows the breathing out.

4. Processing Time

You may hear, "How far is it to "X-Y-Z"?" "Oh, about an hour and a half."

In our fast-paced world, distance is often calculated in minutes rather than miles, time translates to speed, productivity is measured by how quickly the team gets "up and running."

But you often get "up and running" in a completely different way from your colleagues or friends. While you are not inherently slow — nonlinear thinkers aren't typically the first out of the gate — you often *seem to be* the last. That's because your holistic approach to time and your associational logic require you to spend longer at the beginning of a process. This thoughtful ramp-up is called nonlinear *processing time*.

Instead of rushing to action, you familiarize yourself with the elements, establish the context, and build a framework. In general, NLs spend approximately two-thirds of any project time in this initial thinking phase.

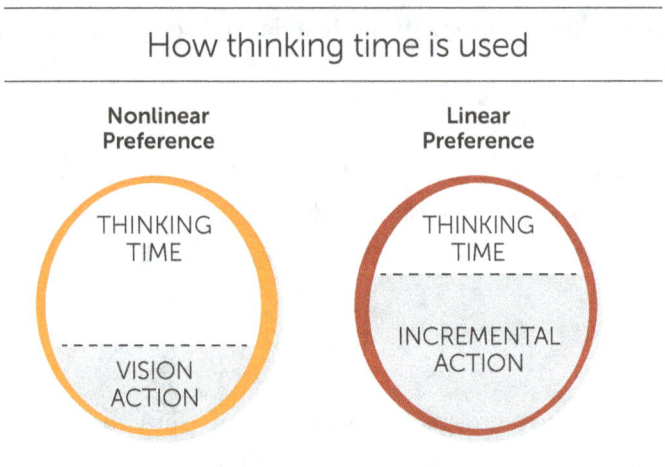

Although linear and NL thinkers often get to the finish line at the same time, they get to that finish line in very different ways.

But that thinking time is well-spent. Your intentional, internal preparation makes your action time intensely efficient. You tend to have less rework and less revising of strategies and tactics. Your *two-thirds preparation* time supports effective *one-third action* on any project or task.

Your linear colleagues work just the opposite way: geared toward quick action and sequential executions, they spend only a third of their project time processing and the other two-thirds on action.

Their quick starts often mean more time is required reworking and revising as they get into any project.

Neither approach is either right or wrong. But to leverage your NL strengths, it's important to understand both approaches. In high-volume, high-tempo work environments, apparent inactivity can look like inefficiency or lack of commitment. *Protect your processing time.* Your "inactivity" is highly productive. It can be the heart of your efficiency. Given a chance, you prove that.

Third NL Distinction: Perception of Time

Summary

As an NL thinker, your holistic and flexible approach to time is a natural extension of your need for the big picture and its context.

Your wide-ranging curiosity and passion for what interests you crowd traditional, linear concepts of time and the sequential demands of its measured minutes, hours, days.

Time becomes irrelevant, and you operate as though you have more than 24 hours in a day. This optimism can wind up putting more on an NL's plate than any human can accomplish, frequently leading to a feeling or an appearance of being overwhelmed or disorganized. Four kinds of time are fundamental to the way your mind works. These four times can be some of your best resources as well as your strongest challenges.

1. *Optimistic time* allows you to be highly productive. It can also leave you over-extended.

2. *Emotional time* gives you an opportunity to infuse your activities with your passion. It can also leave you at odds with colleagues when you lose track of shared time.

3. *Down time* offers you an essential respite from life's daily rush and roar. It frees you to explore or be still without structure or restraints. Others may misunderstand this pause; for you, this is an essential part of creative incubation that helps you right your internal compass.

4. *Processing time* is key to the natural creativity of your NL mind — and is required before you can move forward. It can also be misunderstood in a working world where efficiency is clocked and measured by how busy you look.

Being creative with time is one of NLs' greatest gifts. For NLs, time isn't about hurrying or being obsessively active — or about how quickly or slowly you work.

It's about confidently taking the time you have to work in ways that enhance your unique gifts. ||

Thinking Differently

CHAPTER 4

Fourth NL Distinction

Style of Communication

"Words are not my first language."

— **Brad Pitt,**
actor

Graphic Chapter Overview

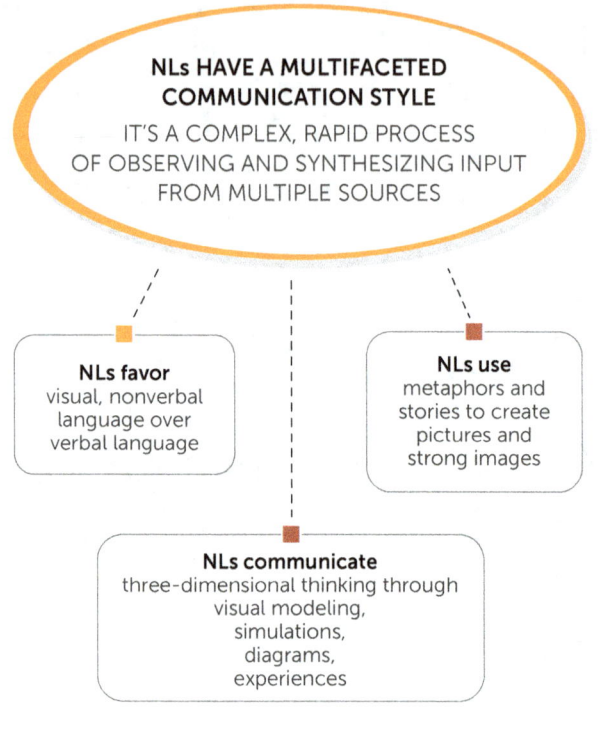

The fourth fundamental distinction of nonlinear thinkers is how they communicate. NLs gravitate to diagrams, graphs, visual models, and stories because they create the connections and breakthroughs that yield NLs' valued explosion of ideas and solutions. These create containers for all that energy of thought and association. Elegant and ingenious, these ways of communicating are *the alphabet of the NL nonverbal language.*

In my years of consulting with NL thinkers, I've worked with entrepreneurs and corporate employees, CEOs, middle managers, functional experts, teachers, students, leaders, followers, and confirmed independents. They're all unique — and they all share definite and predictable processes in their

Fourth NL Distinction: Style of Communication

thinking. And nearly all NLs I have experienced struggle with describing in words how they do what they do.

It stands to reason. In their basic state, words are incremental fragments and sentences are linear strands strung together into sequential narratives. And your way of thinking and engaging with the world is anything but incremental or sequential. NL thinking is a complex, high-speed process of observing and synthesizing input from multiple sources and directions — *almost simultaneously*. Words struggle to keep up. So NLs turn to pictures.

Visual modeling helps NL thinkers understand how complicated things work and how to translate abstract concepts into real-world use. It's not new. Physicist James Clerk Maxwell laid the groundwork for modern quantum physics in the 19th century. He's next to Newton and Einstein in the pantheon of history's greatest scientists. Does it come as a surprise that Maxwell relied on his talents as an artist and sculptor to solve scientific problems? He shaped in clay what he saw in his mind's eye as he worked on a problem.

Maxwell explained, *"If you can visualize the shape, you can understand the system."*

Visual modeling taps into the ability to think spatially. We all do this to some degree. When we find our way around a new city, we use landmarks as well as street names and numbers to orient us in space. For some, a visual map or sketch is better than written directions. On another level, when we pack for a trip, our spatial thinking helps us determine how efficiently we live out of that bag.

NL thinkers, like Dave, our financial planner, create visual mental models as they begin to organize ideas, information, and complex data sets. The models are often three-dimensional, so problems and situations can be assessed and evaluated from different perspectives. Spatial thinking enables NLs to nonverbally use inputs, see pathways through complexity, and identify hidden impacts. Visual models aren't preset structures into which data is forced. Instead, they emerge organically, spontaneously, in response to all kinds of inputs.

This leaning into visual tools reveals one of the most important attributes of spatial intelligence. *Spatial intelligence doesn't have the same limitations as verbal intelligence.* As Elliot W. Eisner of the Stanford Graduate School of Education says, "The limits of our language do not define the limits of our cognition." He sees that the arts have a role in teaching qualitative relationships as well as in understanding complex forms of problem-solving. The arts offer ways to celebrate multiple perspectives. That's good news for mental modelers and artists alike.

Not surprisingly, NLs use visually evocative language — like metaphors — to communicate. NLs frequently conjure up images to add color, depth, and shared associations. Calling a thing something else can be intriguing and speaks to NLs' sense of humor and playfulness. Why say, "My desk is a mess of papers," when you can say, "My desk is a paper parfait"?

This visual orientation can make NLs gifted storytellers. You likely go far beyond simply recounting a sequence of events to draw listeners into the world you're spinning. In captivating your audience, you can actually inhabit the persona of each character in your story.

> *"As I have conversations, I'm making pictures in my mind."*
>
> — **Dylon,** *client*

Because they think so visually and expansively, NLs often have difficulty translating into sequential words the multi-dimensional pictures and models they see in their heads. Their thoughts, which defy the restrictions of shape and form, must be distilled into the funnel of grammar and syntax.

Coming from their visual world, NLs may even start conversations mid-sentence, drawing from the movie in their mind — like a natural spring suddenly bursting from under a rock. The bursting forth can confuse others, unaware that the spring has been flowing silently for miles in subterranean mode.

When Alex, a community relations manager, gets a new idea, she wants to share that excitement with her colleagues. She'll start mid-thought or mid-sentence. But her listeners haven't been in her head. Alex assumes that her team can track her thoughts along with her, holding the entire situation

Fourth NL Distinction: Style of Communication

in their minds and making relational leaps of understanding. "Doesn't everyone think this way?" she asks.

No, they don't.

We're familiar only with our own way of thinking, and we're often so subjective that we don't consider other peoples' equally unique perspectives. Alex's rapid associational logic naturally connects things from multiple sources. The whole picture is clear in her mind. The challenge is to remember that those around her may not be watching the same movie. "I've come up with a name for it," she says: *assumption presumption.*

Your nonlinear talent for visual thinking enhances communication with a speed and clarity far beyond what's possible with words alone. At the same time, that picture or graphic has to interface with words for acceptance and understanding in the linear world. A picture may be worth a thousand words, but the right words applied at the right time can be the difference between a blank stare and the intended *shared* breakthrough.

There are ways to smooth the transition from the three-dimensional, visual structures of your mind to the one-dimensional, literal language of words. This is not done by abandoning your communication approach. On the contrary, it depends on embracing your talents and finding new ways to apply them. We'll explore ways to do this in Chapter 8.

Summary

As an NL thinker, your communications style is a unique, highly effective visual process — observing, connecting, and synthesizing information from many different sources.

To manage the continuous explosion of ideas, thoughts, connections, and inspirations in your mind, you naturally gravitate to pictures and visual models because of their ability — with astounding speed — to give complex relationships a simple, organizing structure. The whole array of visual models you create in your mind can be readily communicated through an adaptable repertoire of diagrams, charts, simulations, video, and stories.

Visual models are the alphabet of NLs' nonverbal language and come first in their thinking. Words may follow to explain the visualizations, but words aren't where NLs start.

Going beyond just recounting a sequence of events, as an NL thinker you often use metaphors to help translate the color and texture of the movie in your mind to connect to your audience.

Your multi-faceted communication style, with its ability to see and think three-dimensionally, is the last of the Four Distinctions that characterize the nonlinear thinker.

The differences highlighted in these first four chapters illuminate the key characteristics of nonlinear thinking and its impact on your life.

Your nonlinear thinking shapes your understanding of the world. It defines what motivates you, how you experience and relate to time, and your visual style of communication. Awareness of these building blocks can help you thrive. They're not random or isolated characteristics; instead, they are an interrelated, deeply integrated system that works exquisitely for how you think.

Yes, you're different. And that's your advantage. ||

Fourth NL Distinction: Style of Communication

Thinking Differently

PART 2

Leveraging Your Nonlinear Thinking

Thinking Differently

CHAPTER 5

Advantages and Opportunities

> *"The keys of the kingdom are changing hands. The future belongs to a different kind of person with a different kind of mind."*
>
> — **Daniel Pink,**
> *author of A Whole New Mind*

Thinking Differently

Graphic Chapter Overview

Thriving in uncertainty and change

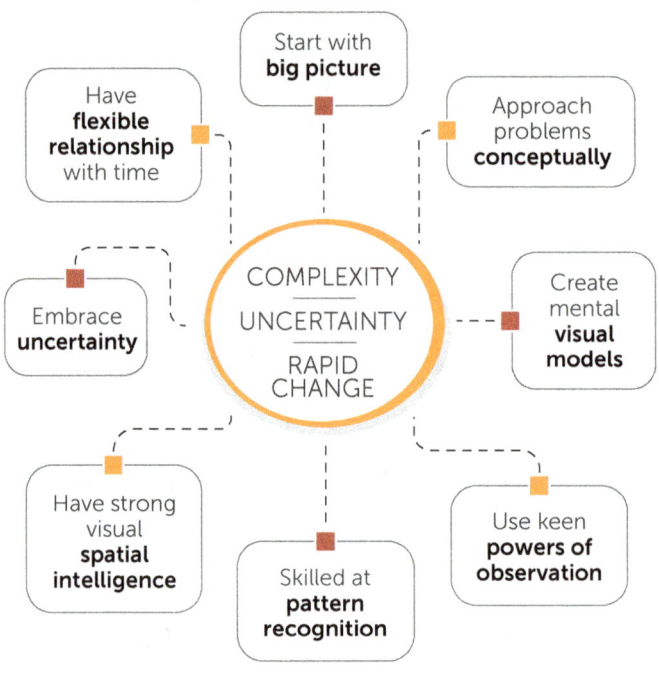

| In a world changing as fast as ours, sometimes just hanging on feels like an accomplishment. Here's some context for that feeling:

The Earth spins on its axis at 1,000 mph at the equator … while it's revolving around the sun at 67,000 mph. The sun, meanwhile, traverses the Milky Way at an even quicker 483,000 mph. With the Earth tethered to the sun by gravity, we go along for the ride, giving a whole new meaning to high-speed mass transit. That's just in our little corner of the world. The universe itself is in motion, expanding at a rate that can exceed the speed of light. And aside from those invisible gravitational tethers, we're not attached to anything.

Complexity, uncertainty, and rapid change are standard components of our daily life. We certainly see it in industry, and not just in a few sectors. Everything from retail marketing to Wall Street is dependent on the ability to navigate and innovate in a constantly changing landscape. In virtually every organization, it's thrive or die.

Those who are going to thrive in this steroid-driven complexity have to be able to process that complexity — and do it rapidly. So many of the world's top entrepreneurs and Nobel laureates see the world in a different way because of their ability to develop and hold opposing traits, values, and ideas and then integrate them into larger ones. Social entrepreneur and business author Michael Simmons notices that some of the world's most innovative leaders see reality in a fundamentally different way. He adds, "People who are able to model how this more complex reality works will be far more successful at navigating it."

Fortunately, as an NL thinker, you're uniquely equipped to thrive in these conditions.

Complexity

As anyone knows who has tried to get a "simple" software update downloaded and synched with his existing devices, simplicity can be elusive.

Within organizations and teams, the more complex a problem is, the more difficult it can be to determine where to begin. For example, how do we sort out overall goals in a mass of available information while also reconciling and integrating competing stakeholders' agendas? You've got a microcosm of spinning, revolving spheres of influence that you have to manage to keep them all from colliding. Having NL thinkers on the team can give a real advantage to any group.

Why?

Here are some of the strengths NL thinkers add:

- **Strength**: *Your proclivity to start with the big picture*
- **Strength**: *Your ability to approach the problem conceptually*
- **Strength**: *Your talent for creating mental and visual models*

These three thinking strengths enable you to quickly organize many disparate elements, avoid unproductive "rabbit holes," and extrapolate connections — all streamlining the path to resolution. These are talents in high demand, ones that are only going to increase in importance and value.

Jordan, our Greenstone River fisherman, was drawn to aerospace engineering because of the complexity of the problems he encountered and their interdisciplinary nature. "Getting an airplane off the ground involves a bit more than getting a car out of the garage," he points out dryly.

Even though he is drawn to solving complex problems, he doesn't like complexity. "I try to find ways that I can step back from a lot of nitty-gritty stuff to look more abstractly at a problem. I start by considering what we're trying to accomplish in order to understand what the problem is before digging into reams and reams of little detail."

> *"If I had an hour to solve a problem, I'd spend 55 minutes thinking about the problem and five minutes thinking about solutions."*
> — **Albert Einstein**,
> developer of the Theory of Relativity

Jordan worked at his aerospace job successfully for several years before taking a completely different career path. He became a technical product manager in charge of metric analytics for a hosted commerce website.

Now, instead of demystifying aerodynamics, he determines which internet pipelines are most efficient and which result in more frequent purchases. He does this by using computer software and color-coded conditional formatting to reveal sales trends. He applies his usual strengths in big-picture orientation, conceptual problem-solving, and visual modeling but in a very different arena.

"I think it stemmed from the stress analysis I used to do as an engineer. Areas of high stress would show up as red. So, in a table of order-pipeline data, if all you have is a table with numbers, it's hard to see anything. But if you color-code it, you start to see discernible patterns. 'Hey, this order pipeline tends to be green, or this one tends to be red.' It's essentially building a topographical map of your problem areas."

The key step for NL thinkers like Jordan is that "step back" to a more global perspective. It sets in motion a whole array of nonlinear talents, including three more of your essential strengths.

- **Strength:** *Your keen powers of observation*
- **Strength:** *Your gift for pattern recognition*
- **Strength:** *Your visual-spatial intelligence*

In short, NLs' ability to integrate, synthesize, and make on-the-spot connections is a real gift, one that's becoming more highly prized for many organizations.

Today, every industry needs NL thinkers who can find elegant solutions amid complexity's cacophony. Visual-spatial thinking is at the heart of this ability to find clarifying solutions. Organizations look increasingly to visual models to clarify the confluence of people and technology. Those models reveal relationships, connections, and challenges more quickly and succinctly than verbal language can.

Visual-spatial literacy is the language of today.

Not that visual-spatial literacy is new — it has long played an essential role in engineering, architecture, economic forecasting, mathematics, astronomy, and the natural sciences. Without visual modeling, breakthroughs in these areas simply wouldn't happen.

But what's new is that visual communication is now everywhere. With the what-you-see-is-what-you-get world of computers, mobile devices and their graphical user interfaces, the 24-hour news onslaught, social media, e-commerce, and general information saturation, we can see virtually anything, anytime, anywhere. The sheer volume of information creates a complexity all its own.

Verbal language simply can't adequately interpret and communicate the layers of this complexity fast enough. Visual-spatial language can.

Who can benefit from your ability to create visual and mental models for organizing these complex layers? Any company or industry that involves people, information, machinery, communication, technology, commerce, time, resources, and costs in any combination.

Another exceptional opportunity for applying visual-spatial literacy to workplace complexity is in risk assessment and management. With a combination of technology and talented visual-spatial thinkers, companies can raise their game by more accurately reading their risks and developing winning strategies.

For example, Mark is a virtual design and construction manager with a world-leading project development and construction group. He helps the company mitigate risk with its projects and personnel by using virtual design and construction (VDC) processes. These include 3D modeling and developing a 4D model that combines the 3D model and the project schedule. On a computer, he can show the construction of a building in virtual space and time. Specialists like Mark are a natural fit wherever the array of components, details, and investments boggles the mind and challenges the bottom line.

In his article "People Who Have Too Many Interests Are More Likely to Be Successful According to Research," Michael Simmons says that those who can learn across fields and combine two or more skills are more successful in this interconnected world. Steve Jobs, who combined tech knowledge with design, is one example. So is Scott Adams, who combined his humor with business observations to give us *Dilbert*. They're polymaths — people who are good at several things — and they use their diverse gifts to revolutionize their fields.

Opportunities abound for such people — green tech, bioengineering, environment, and technology, for example. Or you can create your own new combo.

Uncertainty

Failed major fashion retailers are unhappy indicators of just how difficult that industry can be. Susceptible to the vagaries of uncertainty might define the underlying state of fashion retailing, which is constrained by several factors: complex logistics of global sourcing and distribution;

popular taste that is both highly volatile and deeply subjective; and a marketing landscape that spreads across brick-and-mortar stores, direct-mail catalogs, websites, and social media.

Apparel companies have to be nimble. The ability to anticipate and set trends rather than follow or struggle to catch them is not simply highly valued, it's essential for survival.

> *"I love uncertainty. It means you still have a chance to change things."*
>
> — **Greg,** *client*

Sarah is a keen observer with a gift for pattern recognition. She's an accessories buyer for a high-end fashion concern. Her natural ability to see economic, geographical, and behavioral patterns lets her consistently predict trends ahead of the market. She's in high demand. But to Sarah, predicting trends seems like common sense.

On her travels around the world, she likes to wander through the cities she visits. "I love to get out into the neighborhoods and sit in the squares to watch what people are wearing and doing, what's important to them in their lives."

In Nairobi, she noticed that many schoolgirls wore matching uniforms of blue skirts and white shirts with a brown shoulder bag. But, being teenagers, each wanted to be different, and Sarah saw that each girl had put a colorful design somewhere on her bag that was unique to her.

In Berlin, she noticed a lot of women wearing elaborate tattoos — a change from previous visits. In Amsterdam, she picked up an article on technological advances that allowed customization in cancer care. It triggered memories of the Nairobi schoolgirls and the Berlin women.

Book bag designs. Tattoos. Cancer care. For Sarah, a lightbulb came on: customization, the human desire for self-clarifying beauty. What if that idea could be embraced by the fashion industry? What about "personalized" accessories?

On her flight back to New York, Sarah drafted a pitch for offering customized decoration for accessories at a level not previously considered possible in her industry. Her enthusiasm and precise observation held sway, and she convinced her company that customization was about to become fashion-vital. Sarah was right again, and her company was positioned at the forefront of a huge customization trend in the market.

- **Strength**: *Your ability — and willingness — to embrace uncertainty*

As an NL thinker, your relationship to uncertainty doesn't freak you out, it inspires you. Greg, the project builder who had to follow his curiosity, says, "If everything's a sure thing, you can't affect the outcome as much as you'd like. A guarantee is wonderful. It lets you say, 'I can guarantee a 5% improvement in sales!' But in my experience, it's possible, even probable, that I can get you so, so much more. To me, uncertainty equals possibility!"

Time and again, Greg has proven this to his internet marketing agency clients, upending the model of incremental change. His marketing model, instead, is systemic, flexible, and widely inclusive. So, his solutions adapt to the rapid change that his clients are experiencing — they assess rapid change in real time and adapt to offer more than one solution.

His nonjudgmental data-gathering draws on multiple channels of untapped information. From a wider angle of context, his model investigates the whole system. Then, his *associational logic and visual-spatial intelligence* allow him to build mental models to view the situation from many perspectives and computerize them to show different possible solution paths. Greg's flexible response to uncertainty can leverage rapid, constructive change for his clients.

Rapid Change

In his book *Margin*, physician and futurist Richard Swenson explains that change itself picked up in momentum in the early part of the 20th century and has been accelerating ever since. The reason?

"The mathematics are different," Swenson says. "Many of the linear lines that in the past described our lives well have now disappeared, replaced with lines that slope upward exponentially."

A century ago, change proceeded in such a predictable progression that we tended not to notice it. It lulled us into a linear mindset. We came to expect change only in certain forms, at certain times, and in certain sequences because "it's always been that way."

Not anymore. History has shifted to fast-forward, and the nonlinear, holistic relationship with time and change offers distinct advantages.

- **Strength:** *Your flexible relationship with time*

Kim is a product designer. She's on intimate terms with rapid change and compressed time. As an NL, she embraces it, *approaching time not as a linear progression but as a holistic continuum.* Her design process may start anywhere along that continuum and frequently moves from the future back to the present.

She's less concerned about direction and sequence and more focused on goal and outcome. She envisions what could be and works to make it happen.

"What can we imagine?" Kim asks. "What will it look like? How do we get there? What are the roadblocks? Who are the stakeholders?" Kim's question map is a multi-dimensional process of unfolding possibilities.

"Change challenges me," she says. "It compels me, nudges me, drives me to reach beyond my initial design."

A material she planned to use becomes no longer available. Forced to look for alternatives, she finds a better product. Keeping up with unexpected change isn't a chore to her. She makes it part of her creative process.

Kim needs to be at the forefront of trends and the changing needs of people who will use her kitchen devices. She follows new techniques, explores new materials, and sees how people adapt tools to perform outside their intended use.

> *"I have not failed. I've just found 10,000 ways that won't work."*
>
> — **Thomas Edison,**
> *inventor*

She tucks all this away for future reference. Open and flexible in her process, she can see that information that isn't applicable today might be essential six months later. An experiment that fails miserably today might point to solutions that lead to a breakthrough on the next project. These pieces of information aren't separate; they're all connected.

The NL thinker's approach to time that Kim and other designers use allows them to function in the face of rapid change. It may actually feed that change and speed it further. One of the early uses of 3D printers was in rapid prototyping, enabling 3D models to be quickly and inexpensively built during the design process. Now, 3D printers are revolutionizing manufacturing. It's predicted that 3D printing will have an even bigger impact on economies and society than the internet.

In an interview with *The World Today* magazine, Australian technology specialist Steve Sammartino notes, "We're going to see desktop manufacturing in the same way that we saw desktop publishing and information transfer. We can actually transfer physical products to other people — they'll print it at the other end, just like we would send an email."

3D printers are now used to produce commercial medical devices, as well as parts for automobiles and airplanes. They're being tested in the food and apparel industries. In the future, instead of waiting months for your new home to be built, a giant 3D printer could roll up to your site and build your house in minutes. Outlandish? A Chinese company recently printed an entire house, including wiring and plumbing, in under three hours.

That's rapid change.

Summary

Complexity, uncertainty, and rapid change: these can be wildly intimidating, even immobilizing. And yet that's our world. An NL thinker is uniquely equipped to thrive in this never-static environment.

Here are eight of your essential strengths:
    1. Your proclivity to start with the big picture
    2. Your ability to approach problems conceptually
    3. Your talent for creating mental and visual models

4. Your keen powers of observation
5. Your gift for pattern recognition
6. Your visual-spatial intelligence
7. Your ability — and willingness — to embrace uncertainty
8. Your flexible relationship with time

Bestselling author and internationally recognized neuropsychiatrist John J. Ratey, M.D., of Harvard Medical School has written, "I am firmly convinced that a more nonlinear kind of thought will eventually supplant much of the logical reasoning we use today."

If you're ready, as an NL thinker, you have the ability to keep your feet firmly planted on this rapidly spinning, revolving ground on which we stand. You can do so with aplomb. And in the process, you can *lead the way in manifesting transformative change* wherever you are. ||

Thinking Differently

CHAPTER 6

Classic Roadblocks

"It's not easy being green."

— **Kermit the Frog,**
"Sesame Street" character

Thinking Differently

Graphic Chapter Overview

Challenges can come from how NLs think

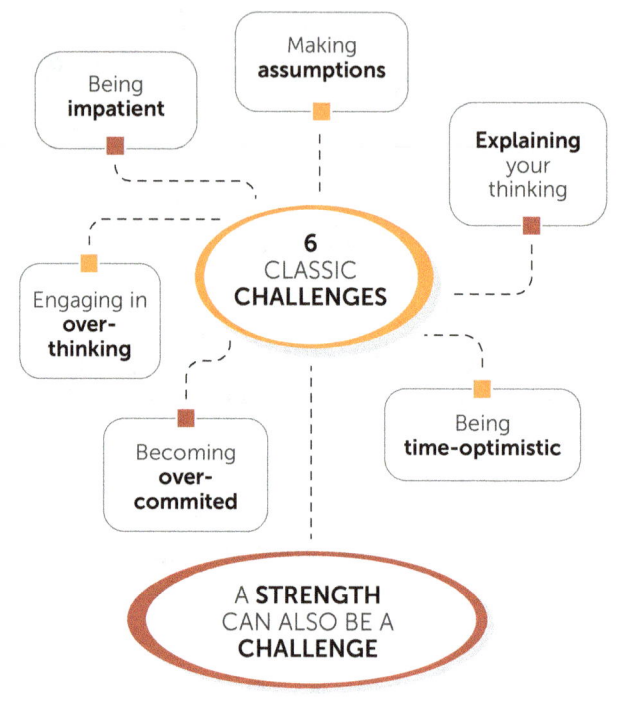

In T.H. White's retelling of the Arthurian legend, *The Once and Future King*, the great magician Merlin is portrayed as living backward in time. Unlike all the rest of humankind, he comes from the future and grows into the past. Foretelling the future becomes a simple matter of remembering what he's already seen. But living in the opposite direction in time from every other living being can be a mind-bending challenge. Merlin has no shared memories, no shared context for understanding the new or unfamiliar, no shared frame of reference. That can be a confusing and lonely place.

NLs have a unique set of talents that spring from an equally unique view of the world. You have radar to see trends and solve complex problems, but when the majority of the population thinks linearly, that leaves you faced with real challenges.

And challenges for nonlinear thinkers often also come from the very strengths of how they think.

In working with clients, I have found that while every individual NL has his or her own mix of talents and roadblocks, there are six challenges that consistently show up.

Impatience

Jeff and Li work together. Nonlinear Jeff synthesizes a lot of disparate data. His colleagues respect his ability to see correlations and extrapolate conclusions. Li appreciates Jeff's talent and tries to help him leverage it by giving him what she thinks he needs. She presents him with as much available information as possible, in what Jeff describes as "a data dump."

The information is what he calls "raw" because it comes without context. "I get impatient," he says. "I'm just hearing words from Li — a lot of them — and I don't have any way of making sense of what she has said. It's like a foreign language to me. However hard I try to focus and remember, the information just goes in one ear and out the other. I come away from our meetings with a headache. Li sees my eyes glass over and she thinks I'm not listening to her. That isn't true, but we keep repeating the pattern."

What Jeff needs is a "coat rack."

In other words, he needs a structure on which he can hang the various categories of data in a way that provides him with a context so he can make sense of the information. Without the preliminary structure of that context, Jeff's brain shuts down.

"I get impatient," Jeff says, "when Li explains something over and over again as though I haven't understood, even after I've told her, 'I've got it.' Drives me crazy. It just wastes time, and, to be honest, it's more confusing than helpful. I've already moved on to the next thing while Li is still explaining some detail that's important to her."

This is a classic example of how a natural nonlinear strength — the ability to make rapid leaps of understanding — can also be a challenge. Jeff doesn't need lots of detail and repetition in order to begin making substantial progress. His linear-thinking colleague, Li, on the other hand, needs reassurance that Jeff has "got it." She wants him to repeat the information back to her before they move on. She needs to be reassured that the details that make up the picture for her are noted by Jeff. But he has already begun creating visual models to help him synthesize the data. His impatience rises with each repetition.

Everyone has a unique way of thinking and processing information and a preferred way of receiving it. Li works with sequential facts.

In this instance, Jeff can disarm Li's discomfort and ease her need to over-explain with a few simple words: "Yes, Li, I see what you're saying, and I can take it from here. What do you need from me to feel confident you've gotten through to me?"

There's an expression in the Chinese martial art *taijiquan*, "A force of four ounces deflects a thousand pounds." Just a few words of acknowledgment can deflect the mounting frustration that so often comes with miscommunication.

Making Assumptions

> *"Assumptions are the termites of relationships."*
> — **Henry Winkler,**
> *actor, producer*

NL thinkers' free-form, mental-image style of connection often leaves them in a communications gap with others — *in both their personal and work relationships*. For example, you thought you were planting the garden after the garden show next month, but your spouse thought you were going to start planting it tomorrow. You each presumed you were in agreement — until the next day!

Alex, our community relations manager, had a similar problem at work. She began explaining her ideas in mid-thought. She was working from the picture in her mind, assuming that everyone else was there with her. They weren't. And they couldn't follow her.

How do NLs solve this communications roadblock?

A sentence of overview at the beginning of a conversation can quickly focus others and get everyone on the same page. It doesn't need to be long or reconstruct the entire thought process. Just saying upfront who the players are can often do the job. Maybe your preface is a sketch or a map of interconnected thoughts that flow from the central point. It can be almost anything. But providing your audience with a *transition* and a *context* can make all the difference in how your idea is received.

Articulating Thoughts

> *"Good art provides people with a vocabulary about things they can't articulate."*
> — Mos Def,
> rapper, actor, activist

The more difficult the problem, the better Cory likes it. Working in the field of bioinformatics, which combines computer science, biology, mathematics, and engineering to analyze and interpret biological data, he has opportunities to pursue his passion.

Once he's reviewed the problem and gathered sufficient data, he retreats behind his three computer screens for exploration. Depending on the size and complexity of the problem, a few hours or a few days may pass in this state. But eventually a big, "Yeah!" emanates from behind the screens. Cory leans back in his chair, a huge grin on his face.

"Solving a problem has an adrenaline rush that's like nothing else," he says. Clearly, he likes this feeling.

Once the problem is solved, he passes quickly through the euphoria of success and wants to move on to the next problem. Unfortunately for him, to get the support he'll need to implement his solution, he now has to write up that solution and explain it in detail. This drains his enthusiasm.

To Cory, this is like being asked to re-create the wheel. "My mind has done its thing and has checked out. Having to describe the steps I took and answer unending questions in countless presentations is definitely not my favorite thing to do." He tends to procrastinate with these tasks, putting them at the bottom of his to-do list. He's already done the truly hard and creative work. Doing the linear, more clerical verbal work seems redundant, blocking his enthusiasm and progress.

Like many NLs, Cory has a hard time putting his mental modeling into words — a language that is, by its nature, one-dimensional, linear, and sequential. His resistance has a price.

Cory drags his feet as he struggles to articulate his process. Because he wants to get on to the next challenge, he doesn't talk about his successes or dwell on them, so he often doesn't get credit for his work. Frequently, it's his manager, who presents Cory's work, who gets the praise and even the promotion — not the problem-solver, Cory.

Cory says, "In fourth grade, I was the only student in the class to get the right answer in math, but when I was asked to describe how I'd come up with the answer, I had no words — my mind was blank. Since I couldn't recall the connections, it was assumed that I'd gotten the answer 'illegally.'"

Time-Optimistic

> *"How did it get so late so soon?"*
>
> — **Dr. Seuss,**
> *children's book author*

John, a member of our book club, arrives at my door precisely at 7 p.m. for the start of the meeting. In the 10 years I've known him, he has been as reliable as Greenwich Mean Time. Another member takes "seven o'clock" as an approximate intention and arrives at 7:15, 7:30, or 8! Like these book club members, people respond to time differently. Their way of thinking can play a part in their response to time.

Life frequently demands that we compartmentalize our thinking to a 30-minute meeting or a 45-minute class. The nonlinear mind finds this arbitrary and frustrating. Once the NL mind is turned on and is in the throes of making rapid associations, it doesn't want to stop.

Many NLs fear that if they interrupt the flow to address some other task or topic, they will forget all their thinking and the associations they've been holding. John, for example, is time-realistic: he can compartmentalize his activity and stop what he's doing without angst because he knows he can dial back to what he was doing and pick up exactly where he left off.

But NLs who are *time-optimistic* respond much differently.

Matt is an example of that NL time challenge. As a graphic designer, he's known by his team for giving well-thought-out presentations complete with diagrams that clearly synthesize all relevant information. But the lead-up to those presentations is often not nearly as clear and organized.

He can do all the required phases, *but his focus and energy are highest at the beginning, at the creative stage* when he is thinking about the ideas, about the design and strategy of the overall concept, and curating the information he wants to share.

In his mind, he sees the slide deck and how it all fits together. "This is easy," he thinks. "It will only take an hour to pull it all together, so I can do it the morning of the meeting. The presentation is still two days away, anyway. No rush."

In an ideal world, where he's guaranteed no interruptions, where he would have all the relevant information from all his sources assembled and ready to go in advance, this estimate would be good. But the world rarely works that way. His time optimism leaves him vulnerable to a stressful, chaotic rush in the execution phase, when the linear ability to compartmentalize and prioritize activities in a tight time frame would come in handy.

In our work with time-optimistic thinkers at CereCore Institute, we've tested and proven a good rule of thumb for avoiding time overruns. *Start with your original estimate of how long something will take and then triple the estimate.* No kidding. Triple it.

Thinking Differently

Over-Commitment

> *"There are days where I lose track of time, of place, of everything else because I've been transported to another universe."*
>
> — **Susan Isaacs,**
> *novelist, essayist, screenwriter*

At his startup, when Jason is working on a project that's of high interest to him, he doesn't feel the fatigue that his colleagues do. He can stay focused and intent for hours. He's often the last person to go home. "I just want to work on this a little bit more," he tells team members as they pass his workstation on their way out the door. It's a sign that he's immersed in the passion for the project: *time becomes irrelevant.*

He's a founding member of a successful startup, and he's put in the long hours of dedicated effort this entails. He over-commits himself at times, and a cascade of predictable negatives follows: the quality of his work suffers, which leads to frustration and professional disappointment, and then come challenges in living up to his family obligations.

On the flip side, he can be detached and indifferent toward projects that don't truly engage him. "I can't keep my focus and engagement in meetings where a lot of details are being discussed that don't relate to my area."

As a result, Jason has learned to ask questions. "If I'm starting to get lost in a meeting that's focused on a whole lot of details, it really helps to call a halt and ask, 'I can see all this is important, but can you tell me what the big picture is that you're working toward?' I'll probably add, 'And what do you need from me?' Just that little bit gives me an anchor, so I'm not just floating in a sea of details. As a nonlinear, I get what I need, and they get what they need from me because I've been able to stay connected."

Over-Thinking

Kendal is from Montana, and she takes a "Big Sky Country" approach to problem-solving and risk management. When she sets out to think about a problem and its solution, she considers it more broadly than most people. She does her research. Thoroughly. She integrates all the possible pros and cons, all the what-ifs and why-nots. "Making the right choice constantly changes because it depends on how the situation itself changes and varies. But my colleagues expect the one best solution with the least risk."

Because of her broad view, Kendal is slowed down by overanalyzing benefits and possible risks. She gets drawn into this rabbit hole because she reflexively moves into the mental gymnastics of coming up with a stream of viable options. But when Kendal's mind goes into this hyperdrive, over-thinking can create problems: unnecessary delays, over-complicated explanations, frustrations for herself, her team and her client — all making her appear indecisive.

> *"Too much thinking leads to paralysis by analysis."*
>
> — **Robert Herjavec,**
> *"Shark Tank" star, CEO of global security firm Herjavec Group*

Because Kendal's brain automatically thinks beyond what her client sees, she needs to present solutions in two different categories: the answers the client specifically asked for *and then — and only then —* any additional options Kendal can see from her broader, more future-oriented viewpoint. Kendal can change the communications equation completely by asking more specific questions at the beginning of the project to better clarify the client's current underlying issues. Until the client gets his immediate question answered, he actually can't even hear or process Kendal's broader view, even though it may ultimately serve him better.

Summary

Jeff, Alex, Cory, Matt, Jason, and Kendal bumped up against challenges because of how they think. *Their strengths have also been their challenges.* But they can reduce the obstructive effects with the right strategies. That becomes their one central challenge — to use the strategies that allow their strengths to be strengths while outwitting their roadblocks and speed bumps. You may not be Merlin, but you can still work what looks like magic in your life.

A strength can be a challenge

STRENGTH	CHALLENGE
See whole picture rapidly and have leaps of understanding	Impatient, want to move faster than others
See the big picture clearly in mind	Assume others can do the same
Able to create complex visual and mental models	Explain these mental models sequentially for linear thinkers
View time holistically and see many parts	Can be time-optimistic in execution phase
Driven by personal interest and passion	Often overcommit self or have low commitment, depending on personal interest
See many perspectives and possibilities	Overanalyze things: challenge making one decison

Knowing the potential roadblocks with your strengths can help you overcome them from the start.

"Abandon the unskillful" is a wise Buddhist teaching distilled into a simple phrase. The strategies we explore in the next section present ways to elevate your NL strengths while also abandoning the "unskillful" patterns that may have prevented you from consistently performing at your best — and being recognized for it. ||

Classic Roadblocks

Thinking Differently

PART 3

Orchestrate Life Easily and Confidently

Thinking Differently

CHAPTER 7

Breaking Away From Prescriptive Strategies

"The shoe that fits one person pinches another. There is no recipe for living that fits all."

— **Carl Jung,**
psychiatrist and founder of analytical psychology

Thinking Differently

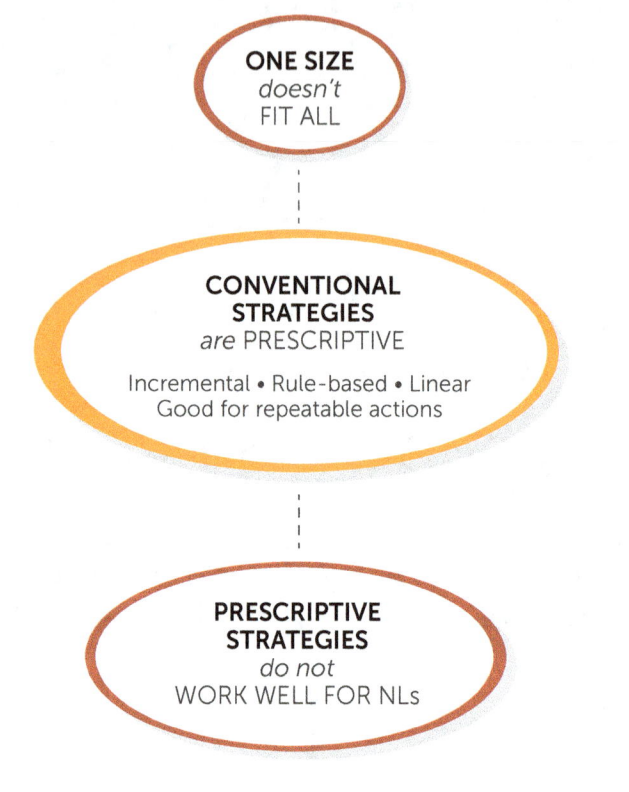

For Abby, success was coming at a steep price. As a senior account manager with a talent management company, she was earning high praise from her manager and clients. They said she was a highly accomplished professional, a trusted adviser, a wonderful partner. But Abby was feeling overwhelmed by her job.

Going to a new client's office always appealed to Abby. There, in those initial meetings, her creativity could really shine. She would start by simply listening to what they needed to meet their goals, both immediately and long-term.

While she was listening, her mind was busy synthesizing the data on many levels. She would also tour the facilities, assessing the work culture and how it could affect her proposal. She would take note of hurdles that needed to be overcome and begin to develop ideas for a creative solution.

By the time she left the client, Abby would have a fair idea of what to initially propose. She could "see" the whole project, and she looked forward to the next meeting, when she would be ready with a well-developed plan.

Returning to her office was a different story.

There, she faced all the background detail and administrative noise that went along with her job. She had to detail, in writing, her excitement and vision for the project. Her initial notes had to be translated for the team into specific written documentation for account reps and recruiters, so they could develop a plan for the follow-up client meeting. On the surface, it appeared that her proficiency and effectiveness continued smoothly.

But Abby's enthusiasm sank under the weight of organizing, prioritizing, and putting into words the vision she had at the client meeting. She found herself procrastinating at getting started, then working more and more evenings and weekends at home to catch up.

She was still meeting her deadlines, one way or another. But it was taking a toll on her and her family. "I was increasingly responding in reactive mode and being less productive." She had always loved her work but found her enthusiasm was waning more and more, along with her output.

When I first met Abby, she had lost all sense of a work-life balance; she was overwhelmed by her constantly growing to-do list. "I'm getting to work earlier and earlier to try and get a head start on the day. I list out all the to-dos on my projects; there might be seven to get done that day, and all of a sudden, it's lunchtime — and only one item done. And 14 more added. I'm not exaggerating — my entire screen can be full."

None of the conventional techniques for time and project management she had been taught were helping. She certainly wasn't being careless with her time, so why was she still struggling?

I asked what happened when she used the conventional strategies.

"With the one-at-a-time strategy, I drop the ball on other projects and fall behind. Some strategies feel cumbersome. I can't think fast enough on my feet to remember which strategy to use or the order of the steps required. Trying to work this way is very stressful. My time is taken up with *managing* the steps and following the instructions." Abby was fighting back tears. "I can't get ahead no matter how hard I try."

The Prescriptive Strategy

Common wisdom says that when things are challenging, you work harder, follow directions, complete the most important task first, and then do the next one. But the limitation of this wisdom is that it's based on a one-size-fits-all assumption, while the truth is, no single approach fits everyone. Abby was fiercely conscientious in following the advice of these conventional strategies — and she was getting buried.

The conventional strategies Abby was using were prescriptive. Prescriptive strategies work well for standard actions that are repeated or performed in a specific sequence, like taking a course of antibiotics in a medical prescription. They work well for linear thinkers because the strategies themselves are linear.

Prescriptive strategies generally involve a formula, a set of rules, written instructions, or standard process that can be memorized and followed each time. A step-by-step process is sequentially linked with clear instructions that can be repeated. Each step builds incrementally toward the final goal, much like the instructions you follow to assemble a bookshelf. These are not guidelines; they're exact steps to follow, trusting the end result will work out.

But Abby is not a prescriptive thinker. She's decidedly nonlinear and highly creative. Very little of what she does at work follows a clean "A to B to C" sequence. The problem-solving she excels at with clients is based on spontaneously using her strengths to freely assess, synthesize, and create solutions.

She didn't suddenly stop being a creative person when she moved from client meetings to her office. But back at the office, her approach was forced to change — sharply. There, she was trying to funnel her nonlinear strengths through linear, prescriptive strategies that were supposed to make her more efficient. But they did the opposite.

Matching Strategy to Strength

Attempting to "go linear" in attacking her in-office responsibilities forced Abby to try to operate in a world foreign to her natural thinking. Like a tropical fruit tree being transported to the desert, she survived, but only by expending nearly all her reserves of energy. It was unsustainable.

When Abby consulted CereCore Institute, it was clear she needed a change in strategy. What if she had a way of "seeing" and organizing her NL mind, a way to convey her vision without losing her enthusiasm under mounds of detail — a way to use her thinking strengths to leverage the same effectiveness back at the office as she did in client meetings?

The idea of intentionally using her natural thinking strengths for in-office management was a whole new concept for Abby. I suggested she use CereCore Institute's Constellation Map, one of what we call our FLEX Strategies — our techniques that help nonlinear thinkers flex to cope with linear, prescriptive structures.

Let's look at how one of these works.

Instead of making her usual lists, in preparation Abby just jotted down her ideas about her project on sticky notes and placed them anywhere on her whiteboard. Then she grouped similar things together.

Now she was ready to ask herself, "What are the most critical topics and issues for this project?" To create the Constellation Map, she identified the main issue from her initial notes and placed it in the center of the whiteboard. Then she began arranging related topics and issues around that focus in a *constellation*. She drew a circle around each of the related groups with a connecting line to the focus. Then dotted lines connected any subgroups.

Freed from the constraints of lists and prescribed steps, Abby found she could create her high-level view and identify the issues for the proposal much more quickly than before. She had them all in one place — where she could see them and how they worked together.

Thinking Differently

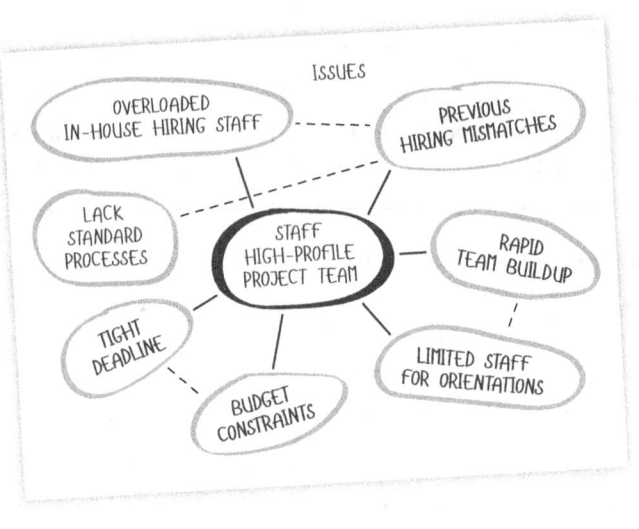

Abby's Constellation Map

Instead of a linear "to-do" list, this visualization of the issues before Abby gives her the instant perspective of groupings and relationships that she needs to make sense of client challenges.

Having a visual structure to work in focused her wide-ranging mind. She was using her visual strength to think about complex information and associations. She found she could hold these thoughts clearly in her mind without listing everything. She now saw the logical starting point just by looking at the diagram. Her associational thinking was in full gear.

This technique is different from what's called mind mapping, in which random ideas are put down anywhere on the board; that can become confusing without the guide of a visual structure. Instead, there was a subtle but strategic difference: Abby was experiencing a strategy that mapped to *her* way of thinking. She had the freedom to work within flexible guidelines. She had a clear picture of the project before getting into the busy thatch of tactics. She was better prepared to communicate her vision and plan with her team. It was also easy to change things as the situation demanded without throwing herself off course — she just removed less important items.

She smiled. "Now I can actually see what my mind is up to." But it was more than just seeing. Instead of getting overwhelmed with lists of things that all seemed to be important, she could see *groupings, connections, and a structure*. She could see where to start and how to create the most efficient sequence of events going forward.

Stepping back and looking at the board again, Abby said, "Seeing things organized in a circular form instead of in separate lists is so much easier." She could now see those *relationships*. She had the whole plan, on one page, ready to share with her team.

A list had never given her this.

Abby began using CereCore's Constellation Map strategy widely. She applied this one-page strategy to projects, team and client meetings, and discussions with her managers because it gave her a way to transform and focus those thousand details into a quick, coherent map.

When Abby was asked to handle the formal proposal for a potential new national client, she was nervous at first because the proposal process was complex and had a lot riding on it. But she was confident that, with her new way of working, she wouldn't get bogged down through the multiple stages of documentation as she had with proposals in the past. Now Abby could turn to her Constellation Map.

"What a relief to see everything in one place! I could see the sections that needed to start immediately, the ones that could wait a bit — particularly those that needed approval by legal or additional manager input.

I identified and managed not only all the components required but also the resources available, including time. I was able to delegate more effectively and be a lot more productive — *all while keeping up with my other responsibilities*. I was amazed. And so was everybody else!"

Abby won the bid, the largest project of its type that her firm had ever managed.

A Constellation Map supported her natural mode of thinking — allowing her to maintain her enthusiasm and energy throughout the project. She used this approach to create great results on other in-office management tasks.

She doubled her weekly sales goals in four months. Even though her past sales were already the highest in her office, she now exceeded the next highest performer by 50 percent. She brought in 31 percent of the office's total weekly gross sales. She sustained that performance over time, increasing her sales by 200 percent in two years!

Abby's passion for her work returned. Her abundant energy and enthusiasm were restored. "And I didn't have to change myself to get here," she said. "Or give up being with my family more. I like that. They like it, too."

Summary

Nonlinear thinkers don't have to work in ways that work against their strengths. Abby needed a different approach for managing her work processes — one that reflected her thinking strengths rather than strategies that were hindering her and making her miserable. While lists may have their uses, like at your trip to the grocery, visual solutions work far more quickly, more flexibly, and more effectively for NLs.

CereCore Institute's visual Constellation Map is a strategy that naturally resonates with the nonlinear process; it can help an NL thinker sidestep the feeling of being overwhelmed and its unwelcome stepchild, burnout.

Breaking away from prescriptive thinking opened the door for Abby's nonlinear thinking to flourish. Once she began working the way her nonlinear mind works, there was no struggle. Being herself was the key to being her best. The transition was smooth, almost effortless.

Abby's experience isn't unique. It's been repeated time and again by nonlinear thinkers in virtually every professional arena as well as in their personal lives. It's an example of how using the right tool for your thinking can change how effective you can be.

The technique she used is actually one of the strategies we've developed at CereCore Institute to rapidly move NLs beyond the speed bumps that slow them down. Because these strategies are customizable by each person and for each situation, we call them FLEX Strategies.

In this next chapter, we will see how just six of the core FLEX Strategies can easily be adapted to common situations.

Breaking Away From Prescriptive Strategies

Thinking Differently

CHAPTER 8

Flex to Change the Playing Field

"I can change the story. I am the story."
— **Jeanette Winterson,**
English writer,
journalist, professor

Thinking Differently

Graphic Chapter Overview

FLEX℠ Strategies enable you to use your strengths and navigate life

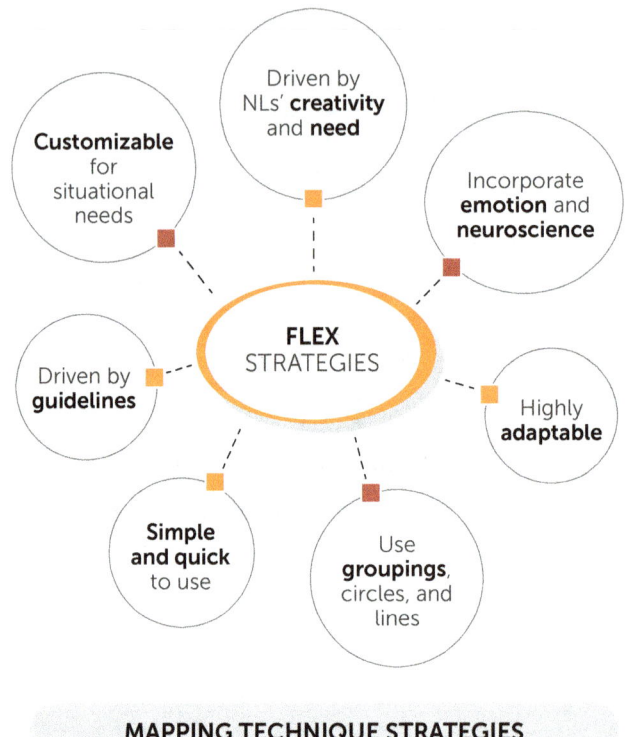

OUR **FLEX STRATEGIES** BREAK THE RULES

- Driven by NLs' **creativity** and **need**
- **Customizable** for situational needs
- Incorporate **emotion** and **neuroscience**
- Driven by **guidelines**
- Highly **adaptable**
- **Simple and quick** to use
- Use **groupings**, circles, and lines

MAPPING TECHNIQUE STRATEGIES

Visual	Balloon Map	**Verbal**	Bridging
	Focus Map		Preamble
	Constellation Map		Discovery Questions

Nonlinear thinkers are wired differently. When it comes to starting almost any task or conversation, they start from a different place. But they have few strategies built for them.

Without the right tools, it can feel like trying to use a screwdriver to do the work of a wrench. By uniting the power of the NL mind with the right strategies, the playing field can be changed.

When we started CereCore Institute, consulting and coaching nonlinear thinkers, we had no trouble finding people who were frustrated with standard operating procedures. From the time they were children, our NL clients had been told, "Complete one thing at a time," "Practice makes perfect," "Follow directions," "If you don't succeed at first, just try harder," and "Vegetables before dessert." Any rule about a sequence for eating food didn't make sense. It was all going to end up in the same place anyway.

The problem for them was that, in the privacy of their own nonlinear minds, they couldn't trust those conventional rules.

They liked finding their own way, as a form of exploring — while doing things over and over had left them frustrated and doing worse at the end than at the beginning.

Their frustration with the rules of engagement was that the rules left them disengaged. Such "rules" are merely strategies that have become calcified. They might work for the vast majority. They don't work for NLs.

> *"For me, prescriptive strategies were like my morning cup of coffee. They wore off after a couple of hours. I needed something that would stick with me."*
>
> — **Dave**, *client*

At CereCore Institute, we developed alternatives to prescriptive strategies. We wanted to come up with tools that were in sync with the unique strengths of nonlinear thinkers.

We had to take a whole new approach to the *idea* of strategies. That meant shaking things up from the very root. We had to throw away the traditional rules-based instructions and replace them with *guidelines and organizing concepts*. We integrated our knowledge of NLs' strengths and needs with the latest neuroscience on brain processing. One more hurdle: the approach had to be simple.

In creating new strategies, we knew that people like tools they can trust, that are reliable, and that work easily. Otherwise, as Abby from our last chapter found, you end up spending too much time managing the foreign-to-you processes and too little time doing the actual work.

The strategies needed to incorporate four core strengths of the nonlinear mind. Therefore, the strategies needed to ...
- be organically rather than sequentially ordered.
- use associational rather than conventional logic.
- use situational rather than rule-based approaches.
- be rapid rather than incremental.

NL thinkers find that structures of groupings, circles, and lines become their best alphabet — the tools on which they can rely to create rapid, non-frustrating results. Why? Because they identify a perimeter, enclose a volume, and convert random data to make it a whole.

When applied to thinking, the big-picture view is a circular perimeter that invites the maximum of free-flowing ideas within it. The circle is an ideal structure for NLs' web-like thinking because at a glance *a circle can encompass the whole picture*, including all its connections and relationships, in a way that sentences and lists cannot.

Abbasid Caliph al-Mansur understood the power of the circle in the eighth century when he commissioned the construction of the Round City of Baghdad. He purposely chose to lay out the city in a circle to foster connectedness and collaboration with the inhabitants and to encourage cross-fertilization of ideas and knowledge. Baghdad became the great learning center of the world at that time.

In our strategies, we connected our circles with lines because lines reveal the *layers* of relationship and connection within and between circles. The specifics of how the shapes and lines are used is open to NLs' creativity.

As part of how NLs work, *emotion* had to be incorporated into the approach. *If a strategy doesn't emotionally engage the NL user, it won't be used.* So, we designed the strategies to be driven by individual creativity and needs

— rather than by a set of instructions. "One size fits all" would not work.

The bar was high for our new strategies. Nonlinear thinkers aren't patient with lengthy to-dos or rigid structures. Strategies absolutely had to be flexible enough to accommodate the ever-changing creative ways in which NLs approach situations.

We came to call CereCore Institute's new approach *FLEX Strategies,* and here's how they're different from standard, prescriptive strategies.

FLEX Strategies are different

FLEX STRATEGY	PRESCRIPTIVE STRATEGY
Nonlinear	Linear
Principle-driven	Rule-driven
Minimal structure	Multiple instructions/steps
Associational logic	Conventional logic
Internally driven ■ Curiosity ■ Personal interest ■ Passion	Externally driven ■ Instructions ■ Pre-set rules ■ Formulaic
Allows for creativity ■ Customization	One size fits all ■ Standardization
Low-threshold access ■ No memorization	High-threshold access ■ Memorize sequential steps
Supports holistic time	Uses linear time

Nonlinear thinkers flourish when they leverage nonlinear strengths rather than relying on linear, prescriptive strategies.

FLEX Strategies are significantly different from the incremental, methodical approach of many prescriptive strategies because they purposefully harmonize directly with your strengths as a nonlinear thinker. These strategies reflect the nonlinear mind itself — capable of exploring multiple scenarios in multiple directions simultaneously, seeing relationships in seemingly unrelated elements, and being creative with process as well as outcome.

These Strategies should not be confused with mind mapping, which has been around for a long time. As we've mentioned, although traditional mind maps are free-flowing and spill out in a stream of consciousness, needed structure is absent in them, and the points required for action are lost.

So, the Strategies needed to be more than what we generally think of as tools. The FLEX Strategies were *created instead to be translators and organizers of the associational mind.* They purposely provide different visual and verbal frameworks so NLs can group, organize, and execute actions before any details are added.

CereCore's FLEX Strategies are quite literally maps of the nonlinear mind. Think of them as a superhighway for navigating the actual terrain of your life.

We knew we'd been successful when clients started flooding us with enthusiastic endorsements and reports on all the new ways they'd found to use our strategies. Some mentioned they even felt guilty about how little effort was needed and how good the results still were.

There are two key types of FLEX Strategies — visual and verbal.

Let's look first at three different *visual* FLEX Strategies. They can be used to organize tasks and ideas. These intentionally flexible designs always start with a framework customized for prioritization, organization or relationship of thoughts. Just the barest guidelines allow you to use and adapt each strategy in the way that works best for your situation.

You can use these tools at work, at home or at school to clarify almost any type of activity. All three are completely adaptable to your way of working and thinking. Here are real-life examples of how our clients use these visual strategies to simplify their lives and manage their time — *without* a to-do lists.

Balloon Mapping: *Prioritizing — the NL way*

Faced with a large project, sometimes the most difficult question to answer is, "Where to begin?" A *Balloon Map* offers an elegant solution by setting priorities and doing it the nonlinear way.

Flex to Change the Playing Field

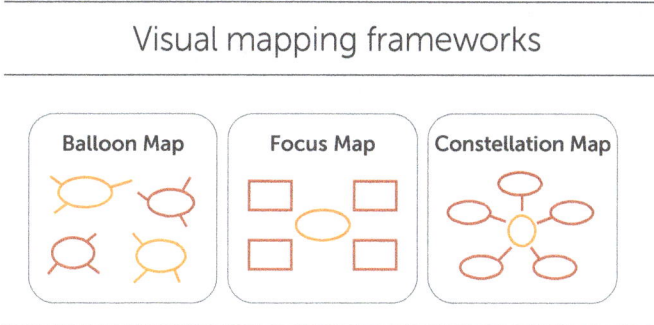

Each type of map has a different application: Balloon Maps prioritize activities. Focus Maps organize tasks. Constellation Maps capture thoughts and their relationships.

In Deb's neighborhood, she's considered the resident plant whisperer. Friends regularly stop by to ask her for gardening advice. The president of the local garden club asked if she'd give a talk on "Gardening for Beginners."

Her mind raced. The challenge wasn't whether she could fill a 90-minute program. It was whether she could pare down the ideas roaring through her mind and organize them. She tried ranking concepts and topics in order of importance. She thought of so many different ways of prioritizing them that she kept tearing up lists and starting over. She saw no way to fit her lifetime love of gardening into an hour and a half, especially with an audience with no shared experience in the subject.

Deb was in the grip of what we call the "Three Ps": procrastination, paralysis, and pain. One evening, she halted the anxious loop going around in her head. "Wait a minute," she told herself, remembering a recent training at CereCore Institute in which she had added a new FLEX Strategy called Balloon Mapping to her repertoire.

She grabbed a small whiteboard she had for grocery lists. On the top third of the whiteboard, she wrote the title of her talk, the garden club name, the date, time, place, contact person name, and email address. Then she began to write in random order, *anywhere* in the remaining two-thirds of open space, all the topics she thought she might want to include.

Freed from having to prioritize her ideas from the start, Deb was able, once

Thinking Differently

again, to experience the creative energy and enthusiasm at the heart of her beloved gardening. She could now approach the talk with that same energy and enthusiasm. The whiteboard filled quickly.

Deb's prioritizing Balloon Map

GARDEN TALK

TITLE - INTRO TO GARDENING
DATE- 2-4
ORGANIZATION- TOUCH THE EARTH GC
CONTACT PERSON- ERIC EVANS
TIME- 7PM
CONTACT INFORMATION
EE@TTEGC.COM
PLACE- COMMUNITY CENTER

7. WORDS OF WISDOM — QUOTES, SEASONED GARDENER
4. PLANTS — PERENNIALS, ANNUALS, SUN, WATER, TEXTURE
1. WHY GARDEN — PERSONAL REASONS, PLEASURE, OUTDOORS
2. DESIGN — WHAT KIND? GARDEN, COLOR, HARDSCAPE, USES, TIME
3. CLIMATE — TYPES, SEASONS, MAINTENANCE, DRAINAGE, SOIL, SHADE
✗ PITFALLS
5. EQUIPMENT — BASIC TOOLS, SUPPLIERS, CLOTHING
6. RESOURCES — BOOKS, WEBSITES, NURSERIES, LOCAL WORKSHOPS

A Balloon Map allows you to download all your random thoughts at the beginning so you can see their relevance and prioritize them later. This helps NLs avoid procrastination.

She jotted down her initial ideas just anywhere on the board. She circled each topic, balloon-style, and stepped back. Immediately, she could see that the balloons weren't random or isolated. There were *associational* links connecting them, and, within those links, an obvious *prioritized sequence emerged*. It felt natural and organic. She numbered each topic balloon in order of importance. She decided that one titled "Pitfalls" was too big a topic for a general introduction to gardening, so she crossed it out. It would make a good follow-up presentation.

Deb had been stressing about this talk for days. And here, in 20 minutes, she had basically designed her whole 90-minute presentation. The central framework was laid out. It looked easy now. Her relief opened the way to relaxing into the talk. She felt her joy in gardening was the most important thing she could pass on to her audience anyway.

Because the framework now was right there on the whiteboard, it could be used as a reference as she worked on her talk. The Balloon Map also made it easy for her nonlinear mind to visually recall the outline as she filled in the details.

Deb's talk went beautifully. She was fully prepared and at ease before her large audience. The garden club invited her to do follow-up talks and in-the-garden workshops.

Balloon Mapping can be used to organize a written paper, school assignment, meeting agenda, a talk like Deb's, or a PowerPoint deck. One simple strategy can work in multiple situations.

The number of balloons can vary depending on the complexity and size of the project, but the process is the same:

- **Capture** the core ideas and components at the beginning, when energy and enthusiasm are at the highest.
- **Purposely write down** the ideas *anywhere* on the page to avoid the paralysis that often sets in when NLs are pressured to prioritize *before they're ready!*
- **Circle the key items.** The "balloons" provide a holding place to gather related ideas together.
- **Write down the actions** that need to be taken, relating them to the content in the balloons.

With the whole project laid out in this way, your NL mind easily detects which balloons don't fit and can be deleted — and how best to *prioritize* those that remain. This final order is established by *numbering* the balloons on the map. With the Balloon Map, your prep work suddenly gets a whole lot faster, a whole lot easier, and a whole lot more fun.

Balloon Mapping is a refreshingly different experience, especially if you've ever struggled with prioritizing. To counteract the pressure to organize and prioritize upfront, *the Balloon Map's flexibility gives creativity and enthusiasm free rein, keeping your energy high.*

Focus Mapping: *The NL "to-do" list*

Abby was determined to approach her family's next vacation differently. She chose a FLEX Strategy from our training to accomplish this — a *Focus Map*. This map provides a framework to capture and organize a wide variety of to-dos as they come to mind *organically* — but not necessarily sequentially.

In the center of her notepad, she wrote her main focus of her trip, San Diego, and circled it. Then she drew four rectangles — her topic boxes — and in each one wrote a key area that needed action: "House," "Work," "Logistics," and "Personal."

As she thought about what needed doing, for each topic box she created task bars around the box. Using action verbs such as "Schedule" and "Call" as reminders for actions to take, she added more tasks as she thought of them.

In just a few minutes, she had an organizing framework for keeping the family and herself on-task for their trip. She didn't have every task written on her map before she started working on the tasks, and she didn't need to.

While she was thinking about her tasks for the "Work" topic box, her mind jumped to a task related to the "Personal" topic box. Without missing a beat, she wrote each task onto the map — *as it came to her.*

She realized that some actions needed to be done first, such as hotel reservations and booking the flights. She numbered these and checked them off when completed. Then she could consider the rest of the tasks as she had time or felt like doing them. *Not having to do them in a set order* but knowing they would all get done relieved her fear that she would forget things. She also didn't have to think about her tasks in a linear structure.

Flex to Change the Playing Field

Abby's family trip Focus Map

Focus Maps are actually a time management tool, allowing you to organize a herd of tasks into one view, simplifying them so you can do them in any order, whenever you have a moment.

This approach helped Abby better deal with the tasks that blocked her emotionally, such as "Pay bills." That wasn't one of Abby's favorite tasks, and it didn't need to be done immediately. So, she moved on to a different one, "Check clothes for trip." That sounded fun, and she got into it with enthusiasm. "And then," says Abby, "when I got to 'Pay bills,' I actually had the energy to do it!"

"Capturing and organizing my to-dos this way makes perfect sense and lets me get more done," Abby beams. "My schedule is already full. I'm on the go a lot and get only a few minutes here and there, waiting for calls or in traffic. But with the Focus Map in mind, it's amazing what I can get done. I can use those little slivers of minutes to work in all the tasks. For example, when traffic was slow, I pulled over and used my cell to stop the mail while we're on vacation. During another, I texted the pet sitter. Check!

Thinking Differently

Done! Instead of trying to do the impossible — make more time — I ended up with time to spare. Amazing!"

Often when we contemplate doing a project, we are overwhelmed by all the many things that need to be done, and the total of them seems staggering. That's especially true for NLs if tasks are in a list. The Focus Map lets you *use your emotion to organize and complete projects instead of forcing your way through a checklist.*

The Focus Map can be scrawled on a piece of paper or whiteboard or posted on your phone or tablet. It works best with a maximum of four topic boxes. If the project calls for more, either the topic titles are too granular or the project is too big and calls for a different FLEX Strategy.

Focus Mapping is also a great way to organize group projects like family chores, for example. In this kind of Focus Map, each person's name goes in a topic box and is posted on the refrigerator or on each person's phone.

A family chores Focus Map

In this example, each person quickly sees their tasks — and they can also see that others have responsibilities as well.

In work settings, the Focus Map is a simple way of laying out individual and team responsibilities for monthly meetings, conferences, or projects.

Constellation Mapping: *Corralling NL thoughts*

Dan is the marketing director for a small company poised to expand its original marketing plan and grow its share in the natural beverage market. In the first two years, the company had grown very quickly because of its young team's high commitment and energy. But the team members hadn't experienced as many industry cycles as Dan.

"I was concerned that we may be too confident going forward," he says. With his NL gift for seeing trends, he was sensing shifts in the market, reflecting changes in the wider culture.

He knew such influences might be overlooked under the pressure of increasing competition and short-term bottom-line demands. His group's strategy meeting was coming up. Dan wanted time to identify critical factors he felt could guide the next stage of marketing.

He took a weekend away. Settling into a chair by the window of his small cabin with the sound of the surf reverberating below, he set out to map his thinking. He had in mind a *Constellation Map*, the same approach used by Abby for her to-do list, in Chapter 7.

On his pad, Dan wrote, "Factors for Next Strategic Plan," and drew a circle around it. This was his central focus.

Around this title, he wrote six key factors that could influence the plan's success. "Seeing these six factors written out this way was exciting," Dan says, "because I knew I could expand my thinking and go beyond just the ones I'd selected and start identifying the web of connections between them."

Dan drew a bold line from each of the six factors to connect them to the central focus. This was the core structure. The dot-dash lines he added reminded him of how the six factors were connected. The dash lines between factors indicated links for deeper consideration.

"I get a lot of mileage from this simple map," says Dan. "By using different kinds of connecting lines or different colored pens, I can quickly identify

Thinking Differently

different relationships or elements to consider."

With his Constellation Map, Dan was now confident that he could communicate the key underpinnings of an effective marketing plan. At the meeting, the map generated a lively discussion. Seeing the connections as Dan had initially framed them allowed his team to make their own associations and add ideas. The meeting became truly interactive. One person said, "I wouldn't have gotten all these relationships or have made sense of them so fast if I didn't see, with my own eyes, where they connect."

Dan's map continued to evolve. His original structure was copied on the computer with dropdowns added for each circle, reflecting insights gathered at the meeting. This opened the framework for further team input. The Constellation Map was integrated into the team's regular arsenal of tools, along with the usual flowcharts and spreadsheets.

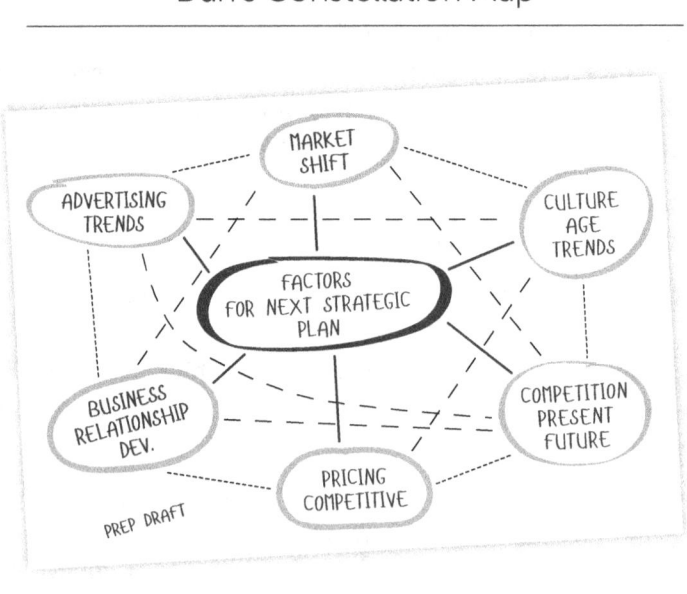

Relationships and connections are too complex for any list, but a map shows the true dynamic of the work ahead.

The Constellation Map's *primary strength is its ability to quickly and clearly identify the central focus along with interrelated connections in a project.* As Dan showed with his creative use of connecting lines, the map can be simultaneously detailed, nuanced, and easily understood.

Not all FLEX Strategies are strictly visual. Three are actually verbal strategies that use words and adjustments in communication styles.

Bridging: *A matter of language and communication style*

The first verbal strategy is *Bridging*, a simple shift in awareness and perspective. It recognizes that the person you're talking to may have a different thinking approach than you and that he may need the *most essential information presented in a different way.*

Deb, our gardener, was in the process of reconfiguring her garden. She had gone over everything that needed to be done with Jerry, her contractor. Or so she thought. She described to him how she wanted the garden to look and gave him the map she'd drawn. She thought everything was perfectly clear.

But Jerry kept calling and texting her with questions. Deb was beginning to get annoyed. But instead of letting that annoyance turn cold, she recalled the Bridging FLEX Strategy.

Deb's natural way of engaging with the world — big-picture, visual, inclined to free-form explorations rather than prescribed sequences — is classically nonlinear. "Unthinkingly, I assumed that my map of changes for the garden — relocating the walkway and reducing the lawn size — would be all Jerry needed since the diagram included all the basic information.

But several days into the work, I realized that we were not connecting: his way of thinking and mine were totally different! "Our missed cues caused me to realize that I hadn't helped him understand what I wanted done. For me to get my garden done properly, Jerry needed information based on *his* way of thinking, not mine. He needed written instructions and to be able to ask me detailed questions about the garden."

Using the Bridging Strategy helped Deb. All Deb had to do was ask Jerry some simple process questions:

- What information does Jerry need?

- How does he need it?
- When does he need this information?

"By using the Bridging Strategy, I was able to speak to Jerry in a way that he could hear me. It's as simple as that," says Deb.

After getting the answers to these three questions, Deb understood what Jerry needed and used that information to help them communicate better the next time they met. When they walked around the garden with Jerry's clipboard in hand, they could more easily verify that they were on the same page with each task. Both were pleased with the garden when it was finished.

Preamble: *Clearly stating the purpose*

The second verbal strategy, *Preamble*, is most useful at the beginning of any conversation when individual thinking styles and communication needs vary. A Preamble *gets everyone on the same page because it does two things:*

- In a few initial words, it introduces the purpose, underlying facts, and scope of a project or gathering.
- It sets the stage for the coming work and creates a tone for collaboration.

For example, had Deb explained to Jerry that the reason she wanted to redesign her garden was because of ongoing drainage problems, this would have eliminated much of Jerry's confusion, many of his questions, and much of their frustration!

A Preamble is not a new concept, but it's a specific reminder that not everyone thinks the same way or can read your mind, so taking a few moments — *early on* — to communicate your intent is helpful.

Discovery Questions: *Getting the context*

The third verbal FLEX Strategy uses *Discovery Questions*. If Deb had asked Jerry key questions at the beginning and throughout the project, it could have fundamentally changed the project's course — both in time and cost. Asking Discovery Questions to really understand the full context of projects and relationships can change the whole equation. With Deb, for example, she could have asked questions like these: "Do you work by yourself or have a team?" "Do you work on one project at a time or several at once?" "What challenges do you see in getting the job done?" "What else do you need from me?" "What's the best way for me to communicate with you?"

Discovery Questions *help you do the following:*

- Inform and build rapport
- Clarify expectations and timelines
- Reveal potential conflicts or challenges
- Understand the full context of any situation

Discovery Questions function in the FLEX Strategies repertoire as a reminder that a relatively small investment of time with *thoughtful queries — especially at the beginning of a project —* can avoid a great deal of misunderstanding, rework, and unnecessary problems later on.

All six FLEX Strategies we've just covered *have four things in common*:
- They're easy to learn and remember
- They're adaptable to a wide range of situations and projects
- They're customizable to match your personal preference
- They're immediately functional

These FLEX Strategies form a reservoir that you can draw from to address the most common situations in everyday life. Rather than bending your habits to suit a structure, the Strategies let you adapt their structure to suit your style and the needs of the situation.

The Strategies may break the rules, but they work for NLs. Professionals, parents, and students can all creatively adapt these FLEX Strategies in navigating their lives.

In the next chapter, we look into the findings in neuroscience that relate to the nonlinear mind and form the underpinnings behind FLEX Strategies.

Summary

CereCore Institute's FLEX Strategies are different from other strategies because they're designed specifically for NL thinkers. The Strategies are the translators of your multifaceted thinking, and they enable you to better organize, communicate, and execute your NL thoughts and actions.

Prescriptive strategies say, "Do this, and you'll succeed." FLEX Strategies operate on the assumption that you, not the strategy, are the key to your success. They harmonize with NLs' true nature and associational strengths while mitigating challenge areas. Another way to say this is that you eliminate the things that make you miserable and transform those same tasks into ones that give you energy and promote your creativity.

The FLEX Strategies are significantly different from the conventional strategies usually recommended. They are designed with the barest guidelines possible. Because of this minimalist structure, there's no steep learning curve. Rapidly, on the first try, they're internalized and usable. These Strategies are deceptively simple.

Because we knew that detailed, incremental instructions would be anathema to you, the Strategies have a simple structure for guiding a project or process through every stage. We wanted NL thinkers to focus their energy and organize their efforts, but we didn't want to intrude on their natural strengths and creative process — or diminish the enjoyment of that process.

Why are FLEX Strategies so transformative if they're so simple? Part of the answer lies in the strength of the tools — like Balloon Mapping, Preamble use, and Focus Mapping. But the real secret is that NL mind of yours! FLEX Strategies are simply access keys — you are the real power source. Use them, and you can change the playing field.

FLEX Strategies are intended to be natural and organic to you. In a sense, they're biodegradable in the way that self-dissolving stitches are in the body: they give support during healing and then are absorbed into the body when the tissues are ready. In the same way, FLEX Strategies create a simple structure to help you practice your craft. Along the way, the structure of the FLEX Strategies dissolves and becomes not an external mechanism, but, in the words of our NL clients, "They are just the way I work." ||

Flex to Change the Playing Field

Thinking Differently

CHAPTER 9

Why This Works

The Science Behind FLEX^{SM} Strategies

> *"Seeking is the granddaddy of the [emotional] systems."*
>
> — **Jaak Panksepp,**
> *neuroscientist, psychobiologist*

Thinking Differently

Graphic Chapter Overview

FLEX℠ Strategies combine neuroscience and psychology with nonlinear thinkers' strengths

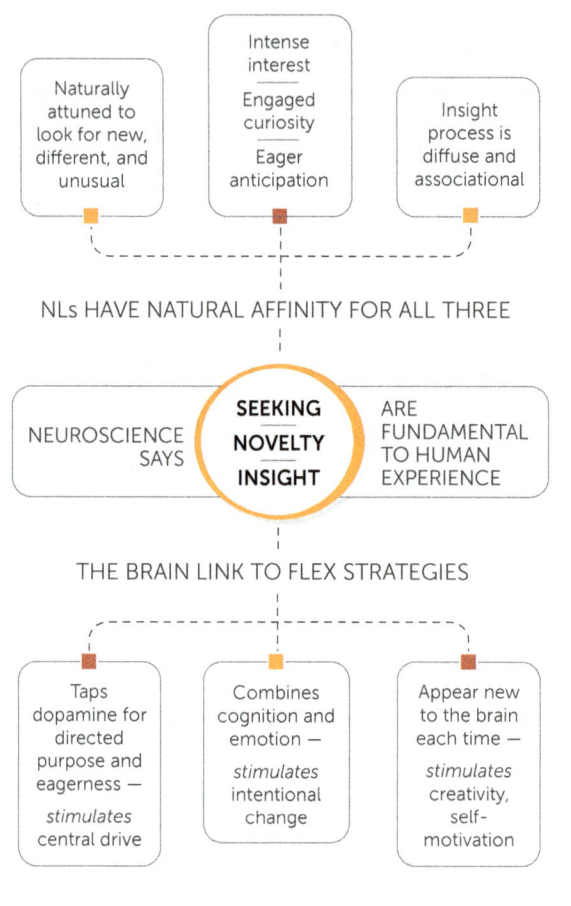

In traditional Chinese medicine, there is no debate on whether the rational mind or the emotional heart is the more reliable guide. Heart and mind are not perceived as being separate. They are *xin, heartmind* — a single, indivisible whole.

Modern neuroscience reveals a similar joined relationship. Cognitive scientist Antonio Damasio, for example, shows in his work how *emotion is essential to reason* and that it's with our emotions that we assign value. The fact is that without emotion — passion, curiosity, and enthusiasm — the mind's innate drive to *seek*, its ability to recognize *novelty* and to gain *insight* simply wither.

These three elements — seeking, novelty, and insight — are fundamental to the human experience. They're how we *learn*, how we *grow*, how we're given the opportunity to *transform* our world rather than simply manipulate it.

For NL thinkers today, seeking, novelty, and insight are especially critical because of the way your brain's wiring affects how you see and engage the world — as we saw when we explored the Four Distinctions.

All the NL Distinctions are coupled with your unquenchable, lifelong curiosity about and interest in the new and different. These core attributes correspond directly to seeking, novelty, and insight. In fact, this powerful transformative trio is integral to the creation of the FLEX Strategies℠.

Let's examine these qualities from a nonlinear perspective and then look at a new way to see them as a whole.

Seeking

Seeking is not simply an action; it's an emotional state. It's the motivational drive that gets us out of bed each day in search of what we need — whether that's our first cup of coffee, a new experience, to change something we aren't satisfied with, or to further a lifelong quest. Neuroscientist Jaak Panksepp, who coined the term *affective neuroscience,* naming the study of the neural mechanisms of emotion, showed that humans can get *just as excited* about abstract rewards as tangible ones. When we get excited about ideas, about making intellectual connections and divining meaning, we use the same seeking circuits in our brain that are firing when we're looking for the perfect cup of coffee.

Specifically, seeking activates the neurotransmitter *dopamine.*

Panksepp found that dopamine circuits "promote states of eagerness and directed purpose." These are states we humans love. They feel good. But more than just activating the reward and pleasure centers of our brain, *dopamine gives us the motivation* to pursue this excitement. Once we have experienced this, we seek out activities that keep the system aroused.

We have an insatiable drive to discover and explore; each personal search invigorates the next. *It's the anticipation of the reward more often than the reward itself that is the primary driver.*

Panksepp suggested that "intense interest," "engaged curiosity," and "eager anticipation" are the types of feelings that reflect arousal of our "seeking system." We all come with these attributes as children. As an NL, you consistently carry these traits of your "child within" into adulthood and throughout your life. These attributes are truly talents and are actively engaged with NLs.

> *"We keep moving forward, opening new doors and doing new things, because we're curious, and curiosity keeps leading us down new paths."*
> — **Walt Disney,**
> creator of the cartoon character Mickey Mouse and The Walt Disney Co.

As an NL thinker, you're a gifted problem-solver for a number of reasons, as we will see. But this talent begins with the fact that you are inherently curious and drawn much more to the process of problem-solving than to the solution. *It's the searching you find exciting,* and while you enjoy successful outcomes, once you have a problem solved, you want to move on to the next one.

Remember Cory, our bioinformatic specialist, with his passion for solving problems? His bane is having to explain himself after the problem is solved. Once he has had the fun of seeking out the solution to a problem, he is in the throes of the adrenaline rush that comes with it, and he just wants to jump right in on the next challenge!

If this sounds familiar, it's not because you or Cory are dissatisfied with your accomplishments. You just have an abundance of passion for exploration.

The anticipation of the journey is what keeps you tuned to seeking and resilient in the face of obstruction or failure. It's what makes you so self-motivated. *For NL thinkers, the fruit of your labor is often the labor itself.*

As we saw before, when we discussed motivation, Leonardo da Vinci combined his limitless curiosity with extraordinary tenacity. He explored an incredible range of subjects to a depth that inspires awe — and then he applied his understandings to everything from flying machines to art. Leonardo, himself, was not attached to his masterpieces as finished pieces. For him, they were experiments in applying the lessons he'd learned: works in progress were a never-ending process. He worked on the *Mona Lisa* for 16 years, right up until his death.

Since NLs need tools that can respond to creative situations, FLEX Strategies, as their name implies, are by intention highly adaptable. They're designed to give your curiosity the free rein it requires, so your anticipation can fuel your drive to explore and seek continuously — in ways that work best for you. The open, organic elements of the Strategies — circles, lines, and empty boxes — are like "mental Legos" that invite NLs to create their own strategy.

In fact, we've found that once introduced to FLEX Strategies, NLs can't resist playing with them because the Strategies stimulate *intense interest, engaged curiosity, and eager anticipation* — the qualities that Panksepp described as being central to the drive to seek.

Although every situation has its own unique possibilities and understandings, each can lead you to apply the customizable FLEX Strategies in new ways. You actually build your own FLEX Strategy every time you use one. You own it, so it quickly goes from a tool to being a partner to becoming an extension of yourself and your creative mind. And confidence soars!

Novelty

If seeking releases dopamine, the neurotransmitter activating the pleasure and reward centers of the brain, how do we engage that energy and potential? What kinds of seeking really get our juices flowing, or will any kind of search do?

The two regions of the midbrain that are uniquely involved in the regulation of dopamine and its relationship to motivation and reward are known as the *substantia nigra* and *ventral tegmental area*. Neuroscientists have found that these regions are especially responsive to *Novelty*, to new information. What that means is *we learn more quickly and remember more clearly* when our brains are stimulated with something *new, different, or unusual*.

> *"The kind of attention we pay actually alters the world: we are, literally, partners in creation."*
> — Iain McGilchrist,
> *psychiatrist, author, former Oxford literary scholar*

As it turns out, NL thinkers' aversion to rote memorization and narrowly structured, repeated exercises isn't simply an obstinate resistance to discipline and order. It's an intuitive leaning into the need for *novelty*. And because your associational logic is especially geared for making connections, even unexpected and atypical ones, *you naturally tend to look for anomalies, outliers, and the unexpected*.

That NL attunement to novelty is a significant advantage because *novelty drives focus* and creates a state of readiness. It grabs our attention, excites it, and holds it. That's transformative. The powerful effect of focused attention is borne out in studies of quantum physics.

Atoms, electrons, and other subatomic particles actually change properties and behavior when observed, especially when that intentional focused observation is sustained. This is a key factor in the neuroplasticity of the brain — affecting its ability to evolve, adapt, and change.

By focusing our attention on some new concept, idea, or connection, we begin building new synapses in the brain's neural net. *People who regularly seek novelty reshape their brain for more novel solutions.*

We saw this with Sarah, the accessories buyer who keeps her observing mind alert to novelty and to the patterns it often reveals. By staying open and focusing her attention in this way, she's developed an uncanny ability to predict trends. In the fashion industry, where she works, this talent is highly prized because it allows her company to get ahead of the market.

From a much different industry, another example showing novelty driving innovation is the British inventor James Dyson. In 1978, Dyson visited a sawmill and observed how large, cyclonic separators were being used to pull sawdust out of the air. It sparked a question for him: could the same idea of cyclonic separation be used in a home vacuum cleaner?

Five years and 5,000 prototypes later, he had a vacuum that not only worked but set a new standard for performance. To date, the Dyson philosophy of taking novel approaches to traditional home appliances has earned his company more than $10 billion in worldwide sales.

Our visual and verbal FLEX Strategies, with their minimal and adaptable structures, *appear new and novel to the brain each time they're used.* They leverage the novelty that NLs love rather than forcing them to endure standard, linear structures that dull the NL thinker's mind. Novelty is the engine for the NL thinkers' creativity, freeing them from the limitations of detailed instructions.

Fear can inhibit novelty's ability to inspire growth and change — fear of the unknown and of change itself. Fortunately, NLs have uncommon resilience in the face of this kind of dwarfing fear. You turn the tables on it and can actually use your comfort with novelty and uncertainty as weapons *against fear*. This flexibility frees you to explore wherever the unknown beckons you.

Insight

The climax of fruitful seeking and focused attention is the *"aha moment" of Insight*. When that moment arrives, it often seems to come in a flash — out of nowhere. But in fact, the brain has been intentionally preparing for the breakthrough. In their study of insight, cognitive neuroscientists Mark Jung-Beeman and John Kounios constructed a precise time and space map of the insight process.

Within their study, they noted that the brain's right hemisphere processes remote, diffuse associations — insight thinking — and sees the world from a big-picture perspective as a connected whole. The left hemisphere processes close or tight associations — analytical thinking — and sees the world in its component parts.

The burst of brain activity during insight is diffuse and associational — oriented especially in the right hemisphere. Using EEG technology, Jung-Beeman and Kounios have found that 300 milliseconds *before* the answer comes, the EEG registers a spike in gamma rhythm, the highest electrical frequency generated by the brain. Gamma rhythm is thought to come from the binding of neurons as the cells distributed across the cortex pull themselves together — expanding the neural net — and entering consciousness as *insight.*

When insight occurs, that new pattern of neural activity registers on the brain's prefrontal cortex. The cells are altered by the breakthrough: they "see" differently, resulting in new interpretations of a situation or realizations about oneself that previously were unknown or unrecognized. We are able to leap into a new way of thinking.

Along with the surge of new understanding brought with insight comes an adrenaline rush of excitement, motivating us to take action. *The dual waves of heightened cognition and emotion give us the confidence and the momentum to make a change.*

With FLEX Strategies, NLs can reset their emotional baseline and can immediately shift to help themselves create that change. The Strategies provide a framework, unfolding insight organically, right in front of you. These aha moments and the exhilaration that naturally follows when we see something for the first time are exciting.

But more significant, with FLEX Strategies, *change is no longer random.* You can actually prepare for and create change.

Each time you use the Strategies, they create opportunities for creating insight. NLs have embraced these Strategies because they're so effective in opening the mind to quantum leaps in understanding, leaps that mirror the leaps of insight in the brain. The insight itself creates motivation.

A new physiological and psychological framework can be established for each NL thinker, allowing NLs to immediately let go of old, limiting strategies. With FLEX Strategies, NLs can then shift to creating change that favors their strengths.

The ability for NLs to initiate and implement intentional, constructive change is the essence of thriving in today's rapidly changing world. For many of our NL clients, the speed with which the Strategies can implement change is stunning.

"How is it," they frequently ask, "that I was able to go out and *immediately* use my FLEX Strategy and get a totally different result? It's like magic!" No, it's neuroscience working in partnership with the NL mind. It's a precise and elegant working fit in which daily work patterns are *at last* matched to the NL mind.

These quantum leaps of change are not just products of new understanding and insight. An emotional baseline shift is created when NL associational logic and emotion are purposely and cohesively joined. This emotional shift, this leap, is internal and instantaneous. In this moment of revelation or discovery, NLs are already creating *immediate behavioral change.*

It's the shared journey of heart and mind.

At CereCore Institute, our research has discovered that when seeking, novelty, and insight are incorporated into a purposeful cycle of change, a self-motivating system is created. It is one that can be repeated by each person at will. The system works seamlessly with the natural strengths of the NL mind. FLEX Strategies are the implementing tools for this system we call the Insight Change Model[SM].

Insight Change Model[SM]

CereCore Institute's Insight Change Model is the result of our search for a broader, natural approach that NL thinkers can use with FLEX Strategies to create change and intentionally direct their lives. The Model exploits the nonlinear abilities to link divergent associations and emotion, to reframe old thoughts and behaviors. It breaks away from the incremental approach commonly recommended in other change models — which is frequently not appropriate for NLs.

Seeking, novelty, and insight form the core of our Insight Change Model with the "mental trilogy" of cognition, emotion, and motivation offering an important supporting role. This mental trilogy is recognized as essential, and all three components are required for learning and change, as shown in the work of neuroscientist Joseph LeDoux and neurobiologist James McGaugh.

In building a process that works with NLs' strengths and their way of doing things, we realized that NLs required these three opportunities to be successful:
- To be a full partner in creating their process
- To make the rules and guidelines
- To have the excitement of making their own discoveries

The process rather than the outcome becomes the focus of the Model. It's a focus that allows nonlinear thinkers to become active participants in the process, participants who get to discover the change and the excitement of it all. The Model offers the understanding and permission to see change differently.

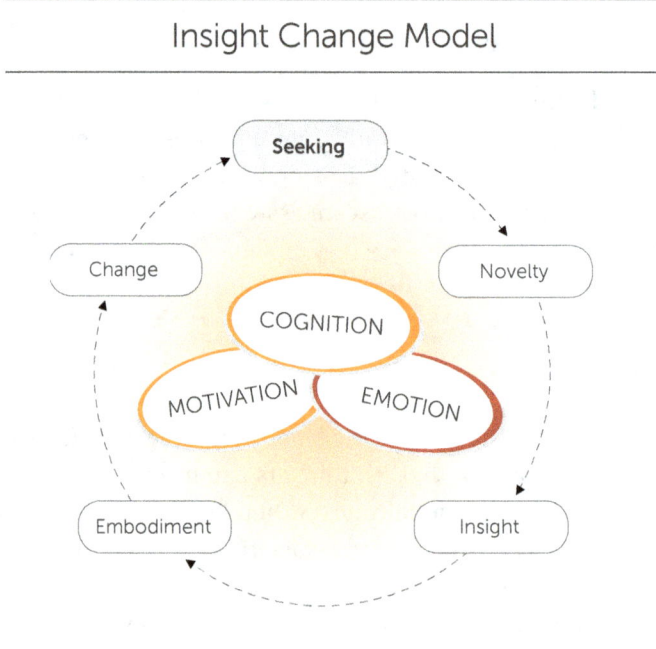

Together, cognition, emotion, and motivation drive the Insight Change Model's integrated, cyclic process of seeking-novelty-insight-embodiment-change.

Rather than following established models, the Insight Change Model puts special emphasis on embodiment and change; that allows NL thinkers to blend all the components in a collaborative way.

For NLs, it's an orchestra of five main components — fluidly interacting and using seeking, novelty, insight, embodiment, and change. The mind combines and uses them, together and separately, as needed to create the symphony of the moment. How does the Insight Change Model actually work?

Seeking: This change model starts with our familiar friend seeking because our motivation to seek is foundational. To carry seeking through the full cycle to sustained change requires engaging nonlinear cognition and emotion in equal measure. Seeking encourages NL attention on process, thus suspending fear of change. That's why NLs have the wonderful ability to rapidly reframe emotional concerns and fears. With fear abated and the search begun, novelty is revealed.

Novelty: In the journey of seeking, novelty attracts the eye and the imagination, engaging creativity and the full thinking process — increasing our readiness, focusing our attention, and opening us to new options and combinations of thought.

Insight: We are then opened to connections and the aha moments of insight, allowing us to *see* things *in a different way*. It is a state frequently marked by an inner certainty of "I've got it!" With this certainty comes a burst of excitement and energy that propels us into the action of change.

Is there a catch? Only that *lasting* change doesn't automatically follow from new insight, however revolutionary or brilliant. That transformation requires further work, which is why *embodiment* and *change* are included as distinct actions in our Model. At this stage, FLEX Strategies are the practical translators of the NL thought, positioned to quickly organize and enable lasting change.

Embodiment: A few words about *embodiment*. Embodiment happens when we take on a change and make it our own. This is essential in all motivation. And since NLs are known to have strong emotional feelings, this is an advantage. Emotion mobilizes and synchronizes the brain. *Without emotion, the idea for change is just that — a nice idea.*

Embodiment emerges for NLs from the excited mix of new insights and their accompanying emotions. Embodiment then reframes the experience, so you can own it and recognize it as a new understanding. This reframing is fundamental to these breakthroughs' becoming grounded in reality.

NLs are independent learners, and they don't respond well to standard, linear preset solutions. NLs want to be fully engaged in the discovery process. So, our embodiment method does not give you the answers. NLs tend to trust their own thinking and context rather than trusting a predetermined set of rules and answers.

Change: The final step in the cycle is change, and NLs can make change quickly. Fortunately, nonlinear thinkers are passionate about new ideas, especially when they have a context in which to understand the new concept. Once NL thinkers have owned the blend of seeking, novelty, insight, and embodiment, they're ready to make immediate change. They don't hold back! And FLEX Strategies help make that change more rapid. Our Insight Change Model mirrors this NL symphony of thinking, this drive to create change — a drive that is essential to NLs.

If embodiment and change are going to be successful, NLs require partnership in the process. You require discovery for yourself. For NLs, this is the whole point of the journey.

For NLs, putting themselves in command of their own change is a powerful rejuvenator. The affirmation and joy that such change brings encourages NLs to repeat this creative cycle over and over again.

Summary

The understandings of neuroscience bring a fresh awareness to the foundations of the human experience. Our approach at CereCore Institute is founded on the core elements of seeking, novelty, and insight but is reframed thoughtfully and differently for nonlinear minds.

This new approach leverages your nonlinear strengths by gathering and allowing the mind to effortlessly restructure thoughts and create rapid change. You access the best of your thinking gifts and can apply them to your personal and professional lives.

Why This Works: The Science Behind FLEX Strategies

Understanding the science behind what you do is powerful and increases your mastery of your skills and talents. The Insight Change Model working with FLEX Strategies, gives you an X-ray into the process that drives those unique strengths.

This knowledge provides you with a vocabulary and ability to own your nonlinear thinking approach. You now know how you think and the best ways to leverage your thinking. You own your space as a nonlinear thinker. Your heart and mind are fully engaged.

You do not have to change who you are. ||

Thinking Differently

CHAPTER 10

Authentic Self-Advocacy

> *"Be yourself. Everyone else is taken."*
> — **Oscar Wilde,**
> *Irish poet and playwright*

Thinking Differently

Graphic Chapter Overview

Aligning your life with your thinking unites heart and mind

THE OPPORTUNITY:

- Enjoy satisfying, rewarding work
- Create inspiring environments
- Build relationships with mutual respect
- Experience the excitement and success of being an NL thinker

---

|| Many of our clients come to CereCore Institute as talented players. Their gifts are immediately apparent. But their passion is often banked, like a fire storing its heat for some later need. The heart isn't fully engaged.

They remain talented players rather than full masters and conductors of their life, responding to outside rules rather than setting the rules.

To think differently is no mistake or accident. Our world is built on the strength of diversity because diverse thinking is integral to the powers of creativity. By opening yourself to understanding how you think — and then adopting simple strategies for aligning your approach with your neural pathways — you have the means to transform your life.

When we align our lives with our way of thinking, heart and mind become united. This is the simplest and most profound form of self-advocacy — practicing the art of living in harmony with our intrinsic nature.

Five Ways to Bridge Heart and Mind

Authentic self-advocacy flies in the face of self-doubt, self-denial, and self-recrimination. By changing those negative patterns, loosening their hold on your decision process, you can seamlessly integrate your nonlinear thinking into your life and convert "challenges" into powerful strengths. It takes only five simple actions:

1. Understand how you think.
2. Position yourself strategically to leverage your thinking — whether that be within a culture, company, role, or project.
3. Learn the language to ask for what you need.
4. Create an environment to support your thinking process.
5. Know the right tools to further your unique talents.

Understand How You Think

Dave, our financial adviser, made an unlikely career choice when he took a job at a large accounting firm. He struggled to reconcile the tight corporate culture with his nonlinear inclinations. To be the full-service financial adviser he wanted to be, he needed specific things to access the whole picture — things to help him work on a project from beginning to end, to enjoy variety and challenge and offer a workout for his love of problem-solving. He couldn't find them in the rigid corporate structure.

But Dave didn't leave the profession; he just left the cubicle. Once in business for himself, he created a working style and environment that felt natural. He transformed his work experience. And he worked on his passion for photography — as a secondary career!

In his spacious home office, books are scattered around in piles. Computers vie for space with photographic equipment. He can see all his materials at once and easily move from one activity to another.

"I can't wait to get in here every morning," Dave says. "I like to leave things spread out so I remember what I was thinking about yesterday and can jump right in. Much better than using the first half-hour figuring out where I was and what I need to do next."

When he runs out of energy, Dave moves to something else. It doesn't have to be financial. "Seems like shifting between projects lets my mind keep working on the first project even while I focus on the second one." He doesn't push himself to complete one project before going to the next. That can be draining — while moving to a different activity invigorates him.

"Before, I just winged it," Dave says. "*Now that I understand how I think*, I'm more confident. I go with my thinking. It's different, and that's perfectly OK. I'm in charge of my life. I know how I work best."

He loves the way he can now make things happen in the way *he* needs to have them happen. "I earn more money than the goal I set when we started this process — and I'm having fun."

Position Yourself Strategically

Once, early in his career, Bruce accepted a job as a systems engineer with a national computer company. He dived into his new role, which was part sales and marketing, part delivery.

"I was excited about new technologies and working with customers, but I had to configure the software after the customer's requirements were established. Turning program requirements into working software was simply hassle after hassle. I wanted to quit my job. I always thought if I worked hard, I could do anything. I couldn't. That was very humbling.

"I also found it hard to make myself consistently follow established processes. My mind was always wandering to how I could *improve* the process and find better ways to accomplish the goals. My manager didn't like this. 'I don't pay you to do extracurricular work,' he said. 'Just do what's given to you, in the way we do it.'"

Where Bruce saw creative ideas and ways to translate them into greater business potential, his manager saw job creep. Bruce decided to go into business for himself. This gave him more opportunity to be creative, but now he had to get involved in fundraising, product development, marketing, and administration. He couldn't move his business forward the way he'd hoped, and he found himself frustrated once again.

Bruce kept looking for his perfect dream job. He even accepted some offers. But none of them was exactly right. What was he missing in all his searches that kept him from finding and landing the elusive dream position?

"I had taken a lot of personality and leadership assessments. But it wasn't until I worked with CereCore Institute and actually focused on how I think and process information that everything clicked. It explained — so much and so accurately — who I am at a deep level. It gave me an understanding beyond just my behavior. It pointed to self-imposed roadblocks, those 'what gets in my way' issues. And, for the first time, it gave me the 'why' of all I'd been through."

The assessment revealed Bruce as a future-oriented NL thinker.

"I was always excited by the possibilities and didn't really focus on what the job requirements meant in terms of the present, day-to-day reality. I didn't think about the culture of the company — it didn't occur to me that the way I work could feel like a threat to someone else. I only saw through my futurist lens: 'Why wouldn't a company want to stay ahead of the market and seize every opportunity?'"

Trial and error had shown him that pre-established processes, ones that limited his involvement, weren't a good fit. Entrepreneurship, requiring too many noncreative administrative responsibilities, was also not right. In previous choices, he hadn't considered whether a new opportunity positioned him *strategically* based on his future-oriented NL talents.

Bruce wasn't an entrepreneur but an *intrapreneur*. He works best *within* an established company but one with a culture grounded in innovation. One that devotes resources of time, money, and professional staff to cutting-edge creative projects as well as to constant improvement. Now that he knows what to look for, he's made the most of his opportunities. At last count, he's created eight successful businesses within large organizations.

Learn the Language to Ask for What You Need

Abby interacts with 12 different groups within her own company. She tried to adjust her communication to each group, which was exhausting. She had never thought about *how* she thinks. Nor did she have words to describe her process for doing her work. She listened to what others said was the way to do things. When this strategy wasn't productive and she fell behind, she worked longer and harder.

Abby, like many NL thinkers, came to CereCore Institute with a fundamental problem: "I don't even know what questions to ask."

Now, armed with the awareness of her nonlinear thinking approach and the language to articulate it, she doesn't have to struggle.

"I am highly visual and need diagrams and written reports — preferably ahead of time — so I can understand the context and have time to process the whole situation." In that one clear sentence, Abby has synthesized her own core strength, what she needs to support it, and her preferred process time. It provides the critical guidelines for her daily functioning and for advocating with others.

Abby uses a *Preamble* to set the context for her communications. This way she ensures that everyone knows the basics. It also helps Abby organize her thoughts ahead of time. Using this strategy helped her solve an ongoing communication problem with her manager.

"People can misunderstand where I'm coming from." Abby says. "They don't all think like me, obviously. My manager definitely doesn't. I used to cause both of us headaches when I'd get charged up about a new idea and rush to his office in the middle of his day. 'Oh, my gosh! Do you have a second? Can I talk to you about this?'

"He's in the middle of something, and I launch into the backstory, so he can see the importance of the idea. Twenty minutes in, he interrupts, 'So, what is the point here?'

"He's thinking I'm getting off track when I'm thinking I'm adding value. He says, 'Can you summarize this for me in an email?' End of discussion.

"Back at my desk, having to reconstruct that 20-minute conversation that I was so excited about and distill it into a businesslike email is *agony*. All he really wants in the email is, 'Per our conversation, I'm going to do X, Y, and Z.' It wasn't that he wasn't listening or that he wasn't interested. I simply wasn't communicating in a way that he could hear me."

Now she sends him a Preamble before a meeting. The Preamble has a short introduction that sets up the purpose, aims, and rationale for what's coming. I do the same thing with my staff and clients.

Abby uses *Discovery Questions* to find out additional information that can deepen her understanding of a situation and discover anything that may be important going forward. For example, when she meets with a new client, she asks questions like these: "Where is the need greatest and why is that the case?" "Do you see this as an ongoing trend or just an immediate need?" "What brought about this need for more team members?" These questions sound obvious, but they help to set the boundaries and deliverables of the project. They often help her clients articulate more clearly what they *really need and want.*

Abby has learned to use her *language as an effective bridge* with her linear-thinking colleagues. She makes sure she gets the big picture, the context, and asks more detailed questions than she did previously. She also takes the time to let others ask her more questions, so they can feel comfortable contributing their expertise. As Abby says. "It seems simple, but it makes a huge difference in how effective I can be at work."

Create Your Own Environment

Location, location, location. Environment matters. It can soothe or energize, inspire or distract. We've talked about the way Dave rebuilt his working space to enhance his natural style of working on multiple things at the same time. Creating an external environment that mirrors the internal landscape of your thinking approach is a powerful ally in manifesting your greatest potential.

Just as NL thinkers differ in the careers they're drawn to, so do the work environments they feel most comfortable in. Dave's walls are filled with both color-coded financial models and favorite photographic images. Abby found that having too much on her walls created a kind of noise. She removed anything that was visually distracting to her, including two large, beautiful paintings: "I needed the white space aesthetically but also functionally for my visual thinking maps." Intrapreneur Bruce likes things out where he can see them. "If I can't see it, it doesn't exist" he says.

Bruce prefers a vertical organization method, with stacks of folders both on his desk and the floor, sorted chronologically based on when he last worked on the item. He deftly manages each visual archaeological dig when he needs a specific bit of information. It amazes his team, but it works for him.

Quiet is also important to Bruce, so his office is out of the main traffic pattern of the company. When he needs to think, he expands his visual field by looking out the window. When he's in action, he turns to his three computer screens so he can see the big picture of whatever project he's working on and at the same time pull up multiple data sheets to compare simultaneously.

Bruce's environment acts as an extension of his mind. Designed properly, it supports his ability to work well.

"My environment is as much a tool for me as my computer," Bruce says.

Know the Right Tools

Up until now, our examples of FLEX Strategies have focused on work and the workplace. But our minds are at work or play 24/7. If you're an NL thinker, that's true at home as it is in the office. Sometimes the most profound self-advocacy and NL creativity come in the theater of our private moments.

There was a time when, if it was Wednesday evening, I would find myself driving across town to the dialysis clinic to visit my friend Stan, one of the most upbeat, optimistic people I have ever met. His optimism flourished even though he had a spreadsheet two pages long of all the surgeries he'd gone through. But now he was dying.

In addition to family and friends, Stan had a small army of doctors and health care professionals helping him. Each held opinions on the therapies he should still consider. One Wednesday evening, overwhelmed by all the advice coming his way, he realized he needed to take charge one last time. Famous for drawing charts and diagrams on any scrap of paper, he reached

Authentic Self-Advocacy

for pencil and paper. He was, after all, a visually oriented NL thinker.

He began building a Constellation Map, drawing a circle in the center of his paper and writing "Quality of Life" in that circle as his main focus. He then started drawing satellite circles around his main focus. That was as much as he had energy for that night, so he set it aside.

The next morning, he woke and began adding circles and a few notes, decoratively enhancing his main point. Most of the satellite circles had to do with the medical procedures and therapies.

With the map, all the individual components and their relationships became clear. Together, they created a quiet space where the noise of all the advice went still and he was able to connect once again to his own deep feelings around the quality and meaning of life — both for him and for those he loved. He was at peace and, at the same time, invigorated.

Stan's Constellation Map

- FIX BLEEDING SOURCE?
  - COLONOSCOPY
  - DIAGNOSTIC TESTS
  - NUCLEAR SCAN
- LONGEVITY BALANCE
- ~~CONTINUE DIALYSIS~~
- BONE DISEASE SHOULDER PAIN THERAPY
- QUALITY OF LIFE
- HOSPICE
- INFECTIONS
  - MRSA
  - C DIFF
- LIVING OPTIONS LIFECARE A.F.H.

Faced with a difficult decision, Stan visualized his concerns and values and brought order to the conflicting noise around him.

Thinking Differently

When Stan's sister arrived, she found the map finished and Stan in good spirits. He told her that he'd already contacted his medical team. "I am clear. I want to spend the rest of the time I have with family and friends. I don't want dialysis or any other intervention."

By using the map diagram, Stan was able to self-advocate in his greatest hour of need. The power of circles and connecting lines helped Stan, and, as it turned out, they helped others as well. The hospice staff had never seen anyone use a map like this before. They were so impressed that they added it to their repertoire of tools to offer families.

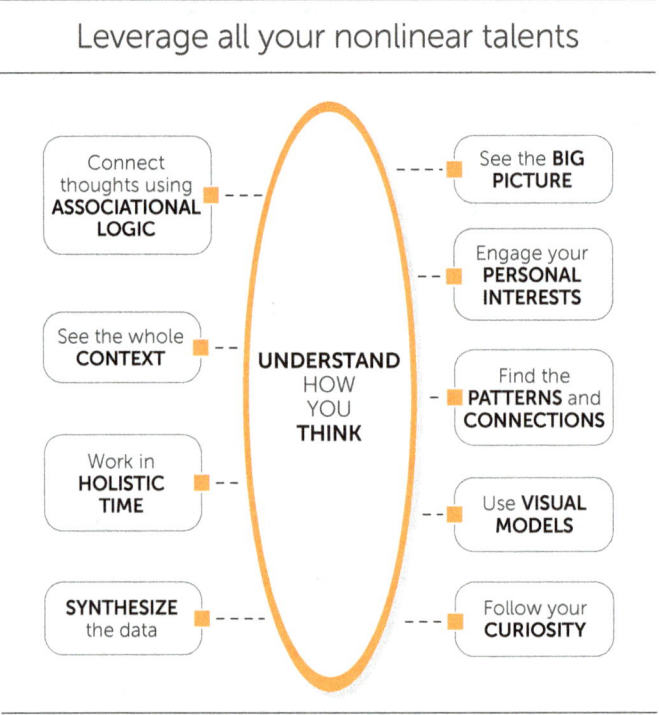

Being aware of how you think allows you to leverage and celebrate your natural nonlinear style and strengths.

Stan enjoyed three weeks of visits from his family and closest friends. My last visit with him came three days before he died. I remember going into his room and feeling the sense of peace that surrounded him. He could barely speak, but his smile, handgrip, and intent eyes enabled us to reminisce over a lifetime of shared joys throughout our work together. It was a goodbye that was pure Stan in every way.

Bringing your wide set of nonlinear strengths and talents to the forefront is key. The FLEX Strategies help you advocate for yourself and vibrantly live your life from the center of who you truly are. Dave, Bruce, Abby, and Stan each found their way to bridge their heart and mind. They are no longer just talented players. They're conducting the symphony of their lives masterfully with enthusiasm and passion.

Summary

When a conductor steps to the podium in front of an orchestra, he's facing a diverse set of options, personalities, talents, and ways of interpreting the music within him.

While the orchestra has to be managed, the conductor can't simply impose his will onto it. He has to lead with his passion and emotion, become in harmony with it as he leads his players in the interactive and shared creation of wonder that his symphony can become.

We have to approach all our relationships with the same kind of dedication, focus, and ability to reveal the vision and passion within us, to self-advocate.

Unless we become the passionate conductor of our life, we abdicate a great deal of our authority and authenticity and miss the true music within us.

For all of us, the first step to creating a harmonious and triumphant result is to understand and embrace how we think. Then we can harmonize with a vast array of personalities, situations, and opportunities. We can find work that is satisfying and rewarding, create inspiring environments to live in, and build relationships based on mutual respect, active listening, and shared purpose. It's work worthy of our finest effort. ||

Thinking Differently

Afterword

For years I've been inspired by NL thinkers, each sharing his or her own intentional way of navigating this unique journey. I hope you have learned from some of them, too, and will seek out and support other nonlinear thinkers you discover in your life's travels.

Your way of thinking is different from the norm, and it's perfect for you. What's more, the "norm" is now changing in response to the world in which we find ourselves, and you are equal to that challenge. You are perfectly matched to thrive in this mix of complexity, uncertainty, and rapid change that fills our future.

Success in your future depends on your taking three core actions.
1. Understand how you think, and act on it.
2. Use tools that support your way of thinking. Flexible minds thrive with FLEX Strategies.
3. Fully engage with your world by skillfully advocating for your needs.

By fully valuing your NL thinking as an integral part of who you are, you embrace an abundance of intriguing possibilities and new opportunities as you conduct your life your way.

I hope this guide provides you with the inspiration and strategies to follow your life's path with courage and boldness.

For my part, I'm so glad I never got to wear that pink tutu. This book might never have happened. But more important, I might have missed a life of learning far more exciting than anything I could have imagined and the joy I've experienced in sharing those learnings with NLs all over the world.

Thinking Differently

Acknowledgments

Thinking Differently is the product of many different peoples' contributions. This book is a culmination of over 25 years of working with both business and individual clients who have generously completed multiple surveys and individual assessments and engaged in both long and short interviews. All have willingly shared their stories, bringing the truth to what it is like to inhabit their life experiences. And in so doing bringing an authenticity to the telling of the NL experience. Thank you, everyone.

A few people deserve special mention.

Without Colin Berg's sage suggestions and editorial wizardry, this book would not have emerged into life. His ability to synthesize many complex thoughts, rein in my big-picture tendencies, and still steward the essence of the book from beginning to end would have made Merlin proud.

Thanks to editor Sandra Eisert, whose drive for excellence and insightfulness shaped the narrative so succinctly. To designer Jason Hoppe for his design expertise in shaping the look and feel of the book. Designer Kate Rappé, for the cover design and for translating the nonlinear mind elegantly with the graphics — all within the restrictions of a linear format. Gillian Levine for her cover illustration inspiration. Mark Stevenson's deft hand in editing the copy. Rebecca Hill, for her work to structure and focus the text. Antonio García Martín's design and color contribution. Bryan Tomasovich for his steady guidance in unfurling the publishing process so patiently and always checking that the needs of nonlinear readers were not being sidelined by the strictures of the publishing world.

BJ Hudgins, program director at CereCore˙ Institute, for her boundless patience and encouragement so graciously given throughout this long project. She always had time for the background discussions, contributing her deep knowledge of nonlinear thinking. She never failed to give thoughtful input even with ridiculously short turnaround times. Robert Neiman, Amy Brewer, Dina Russell, and the late Stan Day for their courage in sharing so honestly and thoughtfully their stories and practical experiences with the FLEX Strategies, which are now all the better for their contributions.

The early supporters of this project need special mention as they encouraged me when it seemed like a mountain too high to climb. Patricia Blumenthal for her belief in *Thinking Differently* as a book that needed to be out in the world, backed up with her lifelong mantra, "Never give up." I heard you. DeeDee Curran, who gently offered just the right words and humor while being a true author's friend every step of the way. Kris Fuller, who brought pioneering neuroscience information to light. David Gallimore's unbounded enthusiasm and generosity of time. Lee Hall, Janis Wignall, and Jeff Reddan, I thank you.

As always, my deep gratitude to my family. To my sons, Morien and Rhodri, for providing a daily nonlinear playground to test ideas, endure assessments, and provide honest feedback. And to my husband, Ivor, whose practical support and patience throughout this journey have been invaluable. He has contributed more to this book than he will ever know.

Acknowledgments

Thinking Differently

Resources

For those who want to explore further, the following resources are grouped based on the different parts of the book for easier access. This is by no means an exhaustive list but a launching pad. Where it takes you from here is up to your curiosity and creativity.

Part 1: The Four Distinctions

FIRST DISTINCTION: Orientation to the World

Bratianu, C. and Vasilache, S. (2009). "Evaluating linear-nonlinear thinking style for knowledge management education," *Management & Marketing* 4(3): 3-18.

Carroll, K. (2017). "Linear and Non-linear Learning." This writing coach makes a compelling case that nonlinear learning is the way we naturally learned for a couple of hundred thousand years. In nature, linear learning doesn't exist. People didn't learn to swim or hunt in a linear way — through a staggered, textbook process. (5 min read). https://ken-carroll.com/2007/12/13/linear-and-non-linear-learning/

Goleman, D. (2005). *Emotional Intelligence: Why It Can Matter More Than IQ*. Bantam Books, New York.

Cook, G. (March 21, 2018). "The Power of Flexible Thinking." Bestselling author Leonard Mlodinow in an interview about his book, *Elastic: Flexible Thinking in a Constantly Changing World*, describes elastic thinking as willing to rise above conventional mindsets, to reframe the questions we ask, to be open to new paradigms. We have to rely as much on our imagination as on logic and have the ability to generate and integrate a wide variety of ideas, to welcome experiment, and be tolerant of failure. (5-10 min read). *Scientific American*. https://www.scientificamerican.com/article/the-power-of-flexible-thinking/

Karandikar, D. "Linear Thinking Vs. Non-linear Thinking: Decide Your Category." In this article on PsycholoGenie, instructional designer Deepa

Karandikar defines linear and nonlinear thinking, including simple examples, the major differences, pros and cons. (5 min read). https://psychologenie.com/linear-thinking-vs-non-linear-thinking

McCumber, C. (2009). "What kind of thinker am I? Linear vs. Non-Linear thinking." In this post, essayist, musician and recording artist Cecil "Chuck" McCumber proposes the following definition: Non-Linear Thinking is human thought characterized by expansion in multiple directions, rather than in one direction, and based on the concept that there are multiple starting points from which one can apply logic to a problem. (5 min read). http://chuckslamp.com/index.php/2009/04/11/non-linearthinking/

Pink, D.H. (2005). *A Whole New Mind: Moving from the Information Age to the Conceptual Age.* Riverhead Books, New York.

Zuckerman, C. (Oct. 15, 2009). "The human brain explained." This science staff writer for National Geographic defines the anatomy of the brain and its functions. Includes links to videos on brain-related conditions such as ADHD, Alzheimer's disease, and depression. (5 min read; videos 2-3 min long). https://www.nationalgeographic.com/science/health-and-human-body/human-body/brain/

SECOND DISTINCTION: NL Motivation

Gino, F. (September–October 2018). "The Business Case for Curiosity" looks at why curiosity matters in business and offers strategies to help leaders increase the ROI in their employees' curiosity as well as their own. *Harvard Business Review.* https://hbr.org/2018/09/curiosity#the-business-case-for-curiosity

Gruber, M.J., Gelman, B.D., and Ranganath, C. (Oct. 22, 2014). "States of Curiosity Modulate Hippocampus-Dependent Learning Via the Dopaminergic Circuit." *Neuro*n 84(2): 486-496. https://doi.org/10.1016/j.neuron.2014.08.060

Isaacson, W. (2017). *Leonardo DaVinci.* Simon & Schuster, New York.

THIRD DISTINCTION: NL Perception of Time

Byrd, D. (Feb. 28, 2013). "Where does our sense of time come from?"

Science educator Deborah Byrd writes, "Our sense of time is mutable, stemming at least in part from our ongoing experience of the external world." (5 min read). https://earthsky.org/human-world/where-does-our-sense-of-time-come-from

Eagleman, D.M., Tse, P.U., Buonomano, D., et al. (Nov. 9, 2005). "Time and the Brain: How Subjective Time Relates to Neural Time." Timing is critical to almost every behavior we engage in, from neural computation to driving a car to playing piano. This academic paper explores the latest neuroscience about how the brain might perceive time. (15-20 min read). *The Journal of Neuroscience. 25(45).* http://www.jneurosci.org/content/25/45/10369

FOURTH DISTINCTION: Style of Communication

General

Forbes, E.G. (1981). *James Clerk Maxwell, F.R.S.E., F.R.S., (1831-1879)*, in *Scottish Men of Science* (series). Edinburgh University Library, Edinburgh.

Silverman, L.K. (2002). *Upside-Down Brilliance: The Visual-Spatial Learner*. DeLeon Publishing Inc., Denver. A wealth of information for parents trying to figure out their visual-spatial thinking child.

Supportive Visual Apps for NLs — Adults and Students

"14 Architecture Games to Unleash Your Creative Mind." A list of some of the most interesting architecture games, which deal with various scales that range from the interior design of the home to the colonization of a planet. (5-10 min read). https://www.arch2o.com/14-architecture-games-unleash-creative-mind/

Kanban Board, a workflow management method designed to help you visualize your work and maximize efficiency. personalkanban.com/pk/

"Mind mapping software." A list of software and apps that aid mind mapping — the practice of connecting "parts" to "wholes" — showing the relationship of related ideas, breaking down larger projects into smaller tasks, etc. (5-10 min read). https://thedigitalprojectmanager.com/mind-mapping-software/

Mindjet Maps for Android is an app based around visuals. You can mind map ideas, take notes, and track tasks with your Android device. It interacts with images, hyperlinks and can access Dropbox. https://www.educationalappstore.com/app/mindjet-maps-for-android

Mindly is a simple, visually beautiful app for structuring, idea collection, and preparing a speech or meeting. You can add colors, icons, and images to the elements. https://www.mindlyapp.com For students, check out https://educationalappstore.com/app/mindly-mind-mapping

Mindomo is a mind mapping app that helps you visually organize your life and improve your productivity through planning and collaborating in real time. Synchronize your maps from any device to the cloud. https://www.mindomo.com For students, check out https://www.educationalappstore.com/app/mindomo-mind-mapping

SimpleMind is a mind mapping tool for your iPad, iPhone, or Android device. Use it for collecting ideas, brainstorming, and visually structuring your thoughts. It has a high rating, a direct link to Dropbox, easy creator usability, and visualization tools. https://simplemind.eu See how students can use this app with their iPads, iPhones, and iPod touches at https://www.educationalappstore.com/app/simplemind-for-ipad-mind-mapping

Part 2: Strengths and Challenges

General

"22 behaviors that creative people exhibit." (5 min read). https://justsomething.co/22-things-creative-people-do-differently-than-the-rest/

Big Think's 2010 interview with neurologist Joseph LeDoux about the role the amygdala plays in learning adaptive behaviors. (5-10 min read). https://bigthink.com/videos/big-think-interview-with-joseph-ledoux-2

Bratianu, C. and Vasilache, S. (2009). "Evaluating linear-nonlinear thinking style for knowledge management education," *Management & Marketing* 4(3): 3-18.

Bronowski, J. (1973). *The Ascent of Man*. Little Brown, Boston.

Buckingham, D. (2007). "Digital Media Literacies: Rethinking Media

Education in the Age of the Internet." *Research in Comparative and International Education.* 2(1): 43-55. https://www.psychologytoday.com/doi/pdf/10.2304/rcie.2007.2.1.43

Darling, N. (2017). "A Pretty Good Organizing System for Non-Linear Thinkers." A psychology professor shares her simple organizing system to help nonlinear thinking people get and stay organized. (<5 min read). https://www.psychologytoday.com/us/blog/thinking-about-kids/201711/pretty-good-organizing-system-non-linear-thinkers

de Langhe, B., Puntoni, S., and Larrick, R. (May-June 2018). "Linear Thinking in a Nonlinear World." Decades of research in cognitive psychology shows that the human mind struggles to understand nonlinear relationships. Our brain wants to make simple straight lines. In business, however, there are many highly nonlinear relationships, and we need to recognize when they're in play. This article shares several counter-intuitive, non-linear business examples. (10-15 min read). *Harvard Business Review.* https://hbr.org/2017/05/linear-thinking-in-a-nonlinear-world A version of this article appeared in the May-June 2017 print issue of the Harvard Business Review, 130-139.

Edison, T.A. (1971). *The Diary of Thomas A. Edison*, a facsimile edition of Edison's July 1885 diary. Chatham Press. http://edison.rutgers.edu/NamesSearch/SingleDoc.php?DocId=MA001

Eisner, E. (2002). *The Arts and the Creation of Mind.* Chapter 4, "What the Arts Teach and How It Shows." Yale University Press. 70-92.

Everitt, C.W.F. (1983). "Maxwell's Scientific Creativity" in *Springs of Scientific Creativity: Essays on Founders of Modern Science.* University of Minnesota Press.

Fuller, J.B., Wallenstein, J.K., Raman, M., et al. (May-June 2019). "Your Workforce Is More Adaptive Than You Think." Boston Consulting Group and Harvard Business School research points to a gap where workers seem to recognize more clearly than leaders do that their organizations are contending with multiple forces of disruption, each of which will affect how companies work differently. (15-20 min read). *Harvard Business Review.* https://hbr.org/2019/05/your-workforce-is-more-adaptable-than-you-think

Gardner, H. (2008). *Five Minds for the Future*. Harvard Business Review Press, Boston.

Judkins, R. (2013). "The Value of Creativity: If you're full of contradictions, value them." This article looks at how a creative person's contradictions are perplexing and frustrating to others and they are the source of their creativity. They can see the world in all its complexity. (<5 min read). *Psychology Today*. https://www.psychologytoday.com/us/blog/connect-creativity/201311/the-value-creativity?amp

McDonald, K.C. (2013). *Innovation: How Innovators Think, Act and Change Our World*. Kogan Page Ltd., London.

Osterman, M., Reio, T.G., and Thirunarayanan, M.O. (2013). "Digital Literacy: A Demand for Nonlinear Thinking Styles." This paper makes the case for a direct link between digital literacy and nonlinear thinking styles, and a demand for nonlinear thinking in education and the workplace. Florida International University, USA. 149-154 https://digitalcommons.fiu.edu/sferc/2013/2013/11

"The Next Episode." (2017). As employers and employees face an ever-changing job market, can nonlinear careers become the new normal? (5 min read). *The Atlantic*.https://www.theatlantic.com/sponsored/jpmc-2017/the-next-episode/1742/

Creativity and Innovation

Farnam Street Blog (2014). "Charlie Munger: Adding Mental Tools to Your Toolbox." Charlie Munger, of Berkshire Hathaway and colleague of Warren Buffet, commends "developing the habit of mastering the multiple models which underlie reality is the best thing you can do." They can help us simulate time (and predict the future) and better understand how the world works and understand how our mental processes lead us astray. (<5 min read). https://fs.blog/2014/11/charlie-munger-mental-models/

Krishnamurthy, B. (2014). "Are You a Linear or Non-Linear Thinker?" Dr. Balaji Krishnamurthy, a veteran corporate executive, posits that organizations that want to engender more creativity need to recruit nonlinear, organized thinkers on their teams. These people can find connections between seemingly unrelated thoughts and then present them in a simple clear way. (5 min read). https://thinkshiftinc.com/leadership-culture/are-you-a-linear-or-non-linear-thinker/

Naiman, L., founder of Creativity at Work (2016). "Adobe Study a Wake-up Call to Invest in Creativity in Business and Education." Global respondents believe being creative is valuable to society (70%) and the economy (64%). People who identify as creators report a household income that is 13% higher than non-creators. 85% of U.S. respondents say creativity makes them better leaders, parents, and students. However, only 31% of respondents feel they are living up to their creative potential, so there is still a creativity gap. (<5 min read). https://www.creativityatwork.com/2016/11/01/investing-in-creativity/

Naiman, L. (2012). "Can Creativity Be Taught?" Research shows that creativity is a natural ability in children. However, adults are affected by the rules and regulations to which they have been subjected in their learning and work environments, so they are less creative than children. Fortunately, adults can become creative through experiential learning opportunities in the right environment. (<5 min read). https://www.creativityatwork.com/2012/03/23/can-creativity-be-taught/

Naiman, L. (2012). "Ideas are the Currency of the New Economy." From Frito-Lay to GE to Hewlett-Packard, there is a clear ROI from the investment in developing employee creativity. (<5 min read). https://www.creativityatwork.com/2012/03/15/ideas-are-the-currency-of-the-new-economy-numbers-tell-the-story/

Naiman, L. (2015). "What Makes Creative Companies Outperform Their Competitors?" More companies that foster creativity achieve exceptional revenue growth than peers. 58% of survey respondents that said their firms foster creativity had revenues exceeding their previous year revenues by 10% or more. More creative companies enjoy greater market share and competitive leadership by a factor of 1.5. (<5 min read). https://www.creativityatwork.com/2015/01/16/creativity-drives-business-results/

Tanner, D., former director of DuPont Center for Creativity and Innovation (2008). *Igniting Innovation Through the Power of Creative Thinking*. Myers House LLC.

VanGundy, A.B. (2005). *101 Activities for Teaching Creativity and Problem*

Solving. Pfeiffer, San Francisco.

Willems, H., co-founder of Image Think (2016). "The Power of Non-Linear Thinking." The lesson shared here for businesspeople and entrepreneurs? Give yourself time away from your work — time to read a book, go for a walk, or to socialize with friends. You are far more likely to prepare your brain for a breakthrough than if you continue to sit at your desk and slog away. (<5 min read). https://www.americanexpress.com/en-us/business/trends-and-insights/articles/power-non-linear-thinking/

Visual-Spatial Thinking

Association of College & Research Libraries (2011). "ACRL Visual Literacy Competency Standards for Higher Education." (>5 minute read). http://www.ala.org/acrl/standards/visualliteracy

Buckingham, D. (2007). "Digital Media Literacies: Rethinking Media Education in the Age of the Internet." *Research in Comparative and International Education.* 2(1): 43-55.

Buenger, V., Daft, R.L., Conlon, E.J., Austin, J. (October 1996). "Competing Values in Organizations: Contextual Influences and Structural Consequences." *Organization Science* 7(5). https://doi.org/10.1287/orsc.7.5.557

McCandless, D. (2009). *Information is Beautiful.* Collins, London. This book beautifully and clearly represents many topics visually. It focuses on the relationship between facts, the context, and the connections that make information meaningful. Example titles: Creation Myths, The Media Jungle, How Clever Are You and Who Really Runs the World.

Silverman, L.K. (2002). *Upside-Down Brilliance: The Visual-Spatial Learner*. DeLeon Publishing Inc., Denver. A wealth of information for parents trying to figure out their visual-spatial thinking child.

Sweetland, R. "*Spatial and Visual Representations, Abilities & Literacy.*" Dr. Robert Sweetland defines and provides a comprehensive set of resources to develop *visual literacy*: the ability to decode visual actions, objects, symbols, and other images and gain meaning from them and to encode thoughts and ideas and express them with visual representations. He also provides a useful list of careers for visual thinkers. (20-30+ min read).

http://homeofbob.com/science/teacherTools/visulztn/index.html

West, T.G. (1997). *In the Mind's Eye: Visual Thinkers, Gifted People with Dyslexia and Other Learning Difficulties, Computer Images and the Ironies of Creativity.* Updated edition. Prometheus Books, Amherst.

Wright, I. (2019). *Brilliant Maps for Curious Minds: 100 New Ways to See the World.* The Experiment, LLC. New York.

Part 3: FLEX Strategies

The Neuroscience Behind Flexible FLEX Strategies

Baddeley, A. (2004). *Your Memory: A User's Guide. (New Illustrated Edition).* Firefly Books Ltd., Buffalo.

Bogen, G.M. (1986). "On the Relationship of Cerebral Duality to Creativity." *Bulletin of Clinical Neurosciences.* 51:30-32.

Damasio, A.R. and Galaburda, A.M. (1985). "Norman Geschwind," *Archives of Neurology* 4(5): 500-504.

Doidge, N. (2007). *The Brain That Changes Itself: Stories of Personal Triumph from the Frontiers of Brain Science.* Viking Adults.

Gazzaniga, M.S. (2008). *Human: The Science Behind What Makes Your Brain Unique.* Harper Perennial, New York.

Gazzaniga, M.S. (2011). *Who's in Charge? Free Will and the Science of the Brain.* HarperCollins, U.S.

Jung-Beeman, M., Collier, A., and Kounios, J. (2008). "How Insight Happens: Learning from the Brain." *NeuroLeadership Journal* 1: 20-25.

Kounios, J. and Jung-Beeman, M. (2009). "The Aha! Moment: The Cognitive Neuroscience of Insight." *Current Directions in Psychological Science* 18(4): 210–216. https://cpb-us-e1.wpmucdn.com/sites/northwestern.edu/dist/a/699/files/2015/11/Aha-The-cognitive-neuroscience-of-insight-2895xqe.pdf

LeDoux, J. (1996). *The Emotional Brain: The Mysterious Underpinnings of Emotional Life.* Simon & Schuster Paperbacks, New York.

McCraty, R. and Zayas, M. (2014). "Intuitive Intelligence, Self-regulation, and Lifting Consciousness." *Global Advances in Health and Medicine.* https://doi.org/10.7453/gahmj.2014.013

McGaugh, J.L. (2003). *Memory and Emotion: The Making of Lasting Memories.* Columbia University Press, New York.

McGilchrist, I. (2019). *The Master and His Emissary: The Divided Brain and the Making of the Western World.* New expanded edition. Yale University Press, New Haven and London.

Modell, A.H. (2003). *Imagination and the Meaningful Brain.* The MIT Press, Cambridge.

Medina, J. (2008). *Brain Rules: 12 Principles for Surviving and Thriving at Work, Home, and School.* Pear Press, Seattle.

Meltzer, P.E. (2010). *The Thinker's Thesaurus: Sophisticated Alternatives to Common Words.* (Expanded Second Edition). W.W. Norton & Co., New York and London.

Panksepp, J. (1998). *Affective Neuroscience: The Foundations of Human and Animal Emotions.* Oxford University Press, Oxford and New York.

Pinker, S.S. (1997). *How the Mind Works.* W.W. Norton & Co., New York and London.

Rock, D. (2006). *Quiet Leadership: Six Steps to Transforming Performance at Work.* Harper Business, New York.

Siegel, D.J. (2012). *The Developing Mind: How Relationships and the Brain Interact to Shape Who We Are.* The Guilford Press, New York.

www.ingramcontent.com/pod-product-compliance
Lightning Source LLC
Chambersburg PA
CBHW071402290426
44108CB00014B/1658